Media, Development, and Institutional Change

NEW THINKING IN POLITICAL ECONOMY

Series Editor: Peter J. Boettke, *George Mason University, USA*

New Thinking in Political Economy aims to encourage scholarship in the intersection of the disciplines of politics, philosophy and economics. It has the ambitious purpose of reinvigorating political economy as a progressive force for understanding social and economic change.

The series is an important forum for the publication of new work analysing the social world from a multidisciplinary perspective. With increased specialization (and professionalization) within universities, interdisciplinary work has become increasingly uncommon. Indeed, during the 20th century, the process of disciplinary specialization reduced the intersection between economics, philosophy and politics and impoverished our understanding of society. Modern economics in particular has become increasingly mathematical and largely ignores the role of institutions and the contribution of moral philosophy and politics.

New Thinking in Political Economy will stimulate new work that combines technical knowledge provided by the 'dismal science' and the wisdom gleaned from the serious study of the 'worldly philosophy'. The series will reinvigorate our understanding of the social world by encouraging a multidisciplinary approach to the challenges confronting society in the new century.

Recent titles in the series include:

Media, Development, and Institutional Change

Christopher J. Coyne

Assistant Professor of Economics, West Virginia University, USA

Peter T. Leeson

BB&T Professor for the Study of Capitalism, Department of Economics, George Mason University, USA

NEW THINKING IN POLITICAL ECONOMY

Edward Elgar
Cheltenham, UK • Northampton, MA, USA

Published by
Edward Elgar Publishing Limited
The Lypiatts
15 Lansdown Road
Cheltenham
Glos GL50 2JA
UK

Edward Elgar Publishing, Inc.
William Pratt House
9 Dewey Court
Northampton,
Massachusetts 01060
USA

A catalogue record for this book
is available from the British Library

Library of Congress Control Number: 2009928598

Mixed Sources
Product group from well-managed
forests and other controlled sources
www.fsc.org Cert no. SA-COC-1565
© 1996 Forest Stewardship Council

FSC

ISBN 978 1 84720 478 3

Printed and bound by MPG Books Group, UK

To Pete Boettke, our mentor, colleague, and friend.

Contents

Figures

Tables

Acknowledgements

In undertaking the research and writing of this book we have benefited from useful discussion and comments from Tim Besley, Peter Boettke, Robin Burgess, Tyler Cowen, James Hines, Jesse Shapiro, Andre Shleifer, Russell Sobel, Bob Subrick, and Richard Wagner. We would also like to thank Alan Sturmer at Edward Elgar for his continued patience and assistance.

Our research on the role of media, institutional change, and economic development has spanned several years. Over that time we have published several papers in academic journals related to the topic of this book. We draw from the ideas in these papers, although this book reflects the fact that our thinking on this topic has evolved since the publication of many of these articles.

Chapter 1 draws on Christopher J. Coyne and Peter T. Leeson (2009) "Media as a Mechanism of Institutional Change and Reinforcement," *Kyklos*, 62 (1): 1–14. Chapter 2 draws on Christopher J. Coyne and Peter T. Leeson (2004) "Read All About It! Understanding the Role of Media in Economic Development," *Kyklos*, 57: 21–44 and Peter T. Leeson and Christopher J. Coyne (2007) "The Reformers' Dilemma: Media, Policy Ownership, and Reform," *European Journal of Law and Economics*, 23: 237–250. Chapter 3 draws on Christopher J. Coyne and Peter T. Leeson (2004) "Read All About It! Understanding the Role of Media in Economic Development," *Kyklos*, 57: 21–44 and Peter T. Leeson and Christopher J. Coyne (2005) "Manipulating the Media," *Institutions and Economic Development*, 1–2: 67–92. Chapter 4 draws on Peter T. Leeson (2008) "Media Freedom, Political Knowledge, and Participation," *Journal of Economic Perspectives*, 22(2): 155–169.

We would also like to thank the Mercatus Center at George Mason University for its generous financial support of this research. We also acknowledge the financial support of the STICERD Centre at the London School of Economics, where we visited as the F.A. Hayek Fellows, as well as financial support from West Virginia University and George Mason University.

1. The big picture: media, development, and institutional change

INTRODUCTION

Following the election of President Alberto Fujimori in Peru in July 1990, Vladimiro Montesinos was named chief of the *Servicio de Inteligencia Nacional* (SIN), Peru's national intelligence service. Prior to this appointment, Montesinos had been a captain in the Peruvian army, an aide to the army chief and prime minister of Peru, and a private lawyer. In his position as chief of SIN, Montesinos served as Fujimori's chief advisor and had nearly unlimited power. Indeed, many considered Montesinos to be more powerful than the President in the daily operations of Peru. In addition to repressing political opponents through threats and violence, Montesinos was also involved in embezzlement, bribery, and drug trafficking. The extent and magnitude of his corruption became evident in 2000.

In September 2000, a videotape surfaced of Montesinos paying a $15 000 bribe to opposition political leader Alberto Kouri to defect and support Fujimori. Shortly thereafter, political opponents of Montesinos aired the scandalous footage. At first the only television channel in Peru to repeatedly broadcast the video of Montesinos's corruption was Channel N, the only private television channel in the country not on Montesinos's payroll. However, as word of the video spread, other television stations, including those previously under Montesinos's control, began airing the video as well.

In addition to his meeting with Kouri, Montesinos had videotaped himself in meetings with judges, political leaders, and members of the media, bribing them as well. Following the broadcast of the Montesinos–Kouri video, these other videos of Montesinos's corruption surfaced and were also aired on Peruvian television. These public broadcasts, which became known as "vladivideos," led to the downfall of the Fujimori regime and the end of Montesinos's reign as chief of the SIN. Fujimori fled to Japan and Montesinos fled to Venezuela. Eventually, authorities arrested Montesinos; he returned to Peru, where the courts convicted him of the "usurpation of authority" and later for dealing in illegal arms.

The fall of Alberto Fujimori and Vladimiro Montesinos illustrates media's potentially pivotal role in checking political abuse. The airing of the vladivideos single handedly led to the demise of Fujimori and Montesinos and their far-reaching web of corruption. The importance of media as a check on government corruption and predation appears even more clearly when one compares the magnitude of the bribes Montesinos paid to judges, politicians, and members of the media.

Economists John McMillan and Pablo Zoido (2004) analyzed these bribes and found that the typical bribe Montesinos paid to a television channel owner was nearly one hundred times greater than the bribe he paid to a politician, which was slightly greater than what he paid to judges. Further, while the typical bribe paid to newspaper owners was less than that paid to the television channel owners, it was still larger than what Montesinos paid to judges and politicians. As McMillan and Zoido conclude, if Montesinos's pattern of bribery tells us anything, it tells us that the strongest threat to government power in Peru was the media.

In addition to highlighting media's role as a check on government actors, the Montesinos story highlights media's potential importance as a mechanism of social change. As mentioned above, the initial video of the Montesinos–Kouri meeting was aired on Channel N, a small private Peruvian cable station, and the only cable channel Montesinos had not bribed. At the time, Channel N had a relatively small market share—less than 5 per cent—with a subscription base only in the tens of thousands (Bowen and Holligan 2003: 332–337). This is probably part of the reason Montesinos did not bother bribing its owners. Despite its small market share, Channel N's decision to repeatedly show the Montesinos bribery video was the catalyst for the Fujimori government's eventual downfall. Political activists overcame Channel N's small market share by setting up televisions in the streets so that passers-by could see the video. Only because Channel N was free from state interference was it initially able to engage in investigative journalism and expose Montesinos's corruption by airing the video. This suggests that even when the state heavily influences the broader media industry, it can still be an important mechanism of change.

Channel N's broadcasting of the Montesinos–Kouri tape initiated a public backlash against the rampant corruption of the Fujimori government. In this sense, the media served as a coordination mechanism for the Peruvian population. The repeated public airings of the vladivideos created common knowledge of the government's corruption, leading to a concerted response against such behavior.

To understand the importance of media as a coordination-enhancing institution, it is important to recognize that the allegations of rampant Peruvian public sector corruption evidenced in the video of the

Montesinos–Kouri meeting were nothing new. Previous accusations, however, often lacked hard evidence, allowing Montesinos to discredit them. As a result, before the public airing of the vladivideos, Peruvian citizens had little incentive to respond in a concerted effort against the Fujimori government's corruption. Any one citizen who considered reacting against the government could not be sure that other citizens would join him. Citizens suffered from a "coordination failure" because they could not be sure what others would do (Weingast 1995, 1997; Hardin 1999). One or only a few citizens reacting against the government would have no effect. Further, if only a handful of citizens agitated for change, Montesinos could have easily identified them and would likely have silenced the dissenters.

The public airing of the vladivideos solved this coordination problem by creating common knowledge of Montesinos's corruption. Because of the repeated media broadcast of the tape, Peruvian citizens could be confident that others knew about the government's corruption, and that these other citizens knew that they knew about the corruption, and so on. Further, the bribery payment shown on the video provided incontrovertible evidence of Montesinos's political abuse. The common knowledge created by the public broadcasts of the vladivideos enabled Peruvian citizens to coordinate on a common reaction to the Fujimori government's misdeeds (McMillan and Zoido 2004: 20–21).

Despite the clear importance of media freedom in constraining the predatory inclinations of government officials and generating the common knowledge and coordination required for social and institutional change, only a minority of the world's countries have what could be described as a genuinely free media. Media freedom is the degree to which governments control or influence the content and flow of media-provided information reaching their citizens. Citizens in developed countries often take media freedom for granted and focus on perceived ideological biases in media reporting (see for instance Goldberg 2003 and Kuypers 2002). However, in most of the world the central issue is not reporting bias but a more fundamental issue of state control of the media in general.[1] In countries where the media is not free, the issue is one of the extent and magnitude of state ownership and government manipulation of the media through threats, bribes, and direct and indirect financial pressures.

Freedom House produces an annual *Freedom of the Press* report that measures media freedom in countries across the globe. The Freedom House index measures countries' media freedom by considering a range of factors: their legal environment, which looks at laws, statues, constitutional provisions, and regulations that enable or restrict the media's ability to operate freely in a country; their political environment, which evaluates the degree of political control over the content of news media in each country (such as editorial independence, official or unofficial censorship, harassment or attacks against journalists); and their economic environment, which includes the structure of media ownership, media-related infrastructure, its concentration, the impact of corruption or bribery on news media content, and the selective withholding or bestowal of subsidies or other sources of financial revenue on some media outlets by the state. The media considered in the index includes TV, radio, newspaper, and the Internet. On the basis of their total scores, Freedom House ranks each country's media as either "Free," "Partly Free" or "Not Free." This ranking provides some means of quantifying the extent to which each country permits the free flow of information and also allows for comparative and trend analysis.

Of course, any attempt to provide an aggregate measure of media freedom will be imperfect and fail to capture all relevant aspects of media that might be important for economic development. For instance, the *Freedom of the Press* report does not take into account the quality of the media or ethical standards of journalists. Despite these imperfections, Freedom House's annual report provides a widely-accepted means of considering media freedom at the global level. Table 1.1 provides an overview of media freedom by region for 2008.

As it indicates, in 33 per cent of the world's countries the media is "Not Free." In another 30 per cent of the globe the media is only "Partly Free." North Africa and the Middle East have the lowest levels of media freedom; 79 per cent of the countries in these regions are rated as "Not Free." In contrast, countries in Western Europe fare the best in terms of media freedom; 96 per cent of the countries in this region have a "Free" media. Further, Western Europe is the only region where a majority of countries have a media rated as "Free." In all other regions, a majority of countries is either "Partially Free" or "Not Free." In terms of population, the 2008 Freedom House report found that only 18 per cent of the world's inhabitants enjoy a "Free" press. In contrast, 40 per cent live under a "Partly Free" press, and 42 per cent live under a press that is "Not Free."

To provide some insight into media freedom over a number of years, Table 1.2 provides time series data for global media freedom between 1990 and 2008.

The data indicate that media freedom, or the lack thereof, has remained relatively consistent over the globe for the past 17 years. Approximately one-third of the world's media has been "Not Free" over this period; a slightly smaller percentage has been only "Partially Free." The data in Tables 1.1 and 1.2 illustrate that for most countries in the world, media freedom cannot be taken for granted.

The absence of media freedom carries significant costs. This was

Table 1.1   Global press freedom by region—2008

Region	Status	Number of Countries	Percentage of Regional Total
Sub-Saharan Africa			
	Free	7	15%
	Partially Free	18	37%
	Not Free	23	48%
Americas			
	Free	16	46%
	Partially Free	17	48%
	Not Free	2	6%
Asia-Pacific			
	Free	16	40%
	Partially Free	10	25%
	Not Free	14	35%
Middle East and North Africa			
	Free	1	5%
	Partially Free	3	16%
	Not Free	15	79%
Central and Eastern Europe (former Soviet Union)			
	Free	8	28%
	Partially Free	10	36%
	Not Free	10	36%
Western Europe			
	Free	24	96%
	Partially Free	1	4%
	Not Free	0	0%
TOTAL – GLOBAL			
	Free	72	37%
	Partially Free	59	30%
	Not Free	64	33%

Source: Freedom House (2008)

highlighted in the World Bank's *World Development Report 2002: Building Institutions for Markets*, which dedicated a chapter to the importance of media freedom for economic and human development (2002: 181–192). The topics explored in the chapter included how a free media could reduce corruption, assist in public health efforts, and improve education. Without a free media, achieving these outcomes is dramatically more difficult.

Table 1.2   Global press freedom—1990–2008

Survey Year	Not Free	Partially Free	Free	Total Countries Surveyed
		Percentage of Total		
1990	46.5	18.2	35.2	159
1991	39.5	21.7	38.9	157
1992	28.4	30.2	41.4	162
1993	28.2	33.9	37.9	177
1994	30.1	33.9	36	186
1995	32.6	33.7	33.7	187
1996	32.1	33.7	34.2	187
1997	33.2	32.6	34.2	187
1998	34.9	29	36	186
1999	35.5	28	36.6	186
2000	35.5	27.4	37.1	186
2001	33.2	28.3	38.5	187
2002	32.8	26.9	40.3	186
2003	35.2	24.4	40.4	193
2004	37.3	24.9	37.8	193
2005	35.6	25.8	38.7	194
2006	34.5	27.8	37.6	194
2007	32	30	38	195
2008	33	30	37	195

Source: http://www.freedomhouse.org/uploads/fop/historical/CBGlobal.pdf (accessed 11 January 2008) and Freedom House (2008)

The importance of media as a mechanism for monitoring government and generating institutional change, coupled with the fact that the media in almost two-thirds of the world is either "Partly Free" or "Not Free," suggests that it is critical to understand the factors influencing the effectiveness of media. The purpose of this book is to contribute to our understanding of media as it relates to economic development and institutional change. Our goal is to analyze the specific factors that constrain the effectiveness of media as a check on government. Further, we explore the process of institutional change and how media serves as a mechanism of change in this process. Our study considers the media in the broadest sense, including the press, television, and radio, as well as more recent media, such as the Internet.

We use economic analysis to explore some fundamental questions about media's role in economic development and institutional change. How is the media connected to the fact that some countries adopt policies and institutions that promote economic development while others fail to do so? What factors influence media's effectiveness as a check on government? In what ways does the government manipulate media to constrain its effectiveness as a check on government activities? How does mass media contribute to the evolution of existing institutions and the adoption of new institutions?

Economic development is a vast topic, both theoretically and empirically. We cannot possibly hope to cover all of its nuances or angles. Our goal is to analyze the role mass media plays in the successful adoption of policies and institutions that foster economic progress. We hope this analysis will contribute to our understanding of one of the many ingredients in the complex recipe for economic development.

ECONOMIC ANALYSIS OF MEDIA AND DEVELOPMENT

The study of media has a long and varied history. The broader field of "media studies" has historically drawn on tools and methods from disciplines as diverse as sociology, social theory, communication theory, literary theory, cultural studies, and anthropology to study media's various aspects. Political scientists have studied media's role in the context of the formation of public opinion and as a means of informing the electorate (see for instance Bartels 1993; Mondak 1995; Brians and Wattenberg 1996). The subfield of "media economics" is relatively young but has increased in popularity over the past two decades. Media economics applies the tools of economics to study the industrial organization of the media and explores both theoretical and empirical questions including media regulation, ownership structures and market share, intellectual property rights, innovation, and advertising, among other topics (see for instance Albarran 2002; Doyle 2002).

We are most concerned with the literature that applies the theories and methods of economics to analyze the connection between media and economic development. This area of research is growing but still in its early stages. The existing literature in this area can be broken into two general categories. The first category focuses on media's role in negotiating the principal–agent problem that citizens confront vis-à-vis their political rulers. It investigates the media as a mechanism that checks government actors. The second category focuses on the economic implications of different media ownership structures. It examines how the features of the media industry affect economic and human development.

Nobel Laureate Amartya Sen (1984, 1999) was the first economist to discuss the importance of media as a means of checking government. He addressed the issue of media in connection to the prevention of famines with a specific focus on India. He notes that "a free press and an active political opposition constitute the best early-warning system a country threatened by famines can have" (1999: 181). His basic argument is that a free press, coupled with an open and stable democracy, pressures political actors to prevent famines. The underlying logic is that in a politically competitive environment, political opposition will have the incentive to communicate the threat of famine to the public to weaken support for incumbents. A free media is the main means of communicating this information to the masses. Failure by the party in power to act will cause a political backlash at the voting booth, leading political agents to better serve their citizens.

For Sen, open political competition *and* a free press are both vital for the prevention of famines. To be sure, media's ability to affect social change is the strongest where the media is free and political competition is vibrant. However, the media can also be an important check on government and an instigator of political change where it is largely unfree and political competition is weak. It is virtually impossible for government to totally suppress the media. At the very least, black market media outlets often persist. As we discuss later in this book, black market media can also help create common knowledge among citizens and coordinate them on political, social, and institutional change. Further, even autocrats have reason to fear the media because of its ability to generate common knowledge about political abuses and, most importantly, to coordinate citizens on responses to such abuse, weakening public support for existing regimes and enhancing citizens' ability to collectively agitate for change. Like the media, political competition in one form or another is omnipresent. Dictators may not face such competition through popular elections. But their position of power is coveted by other aspiring politicos happy to displace them if their support erodes to such a point that displacement is possible. Thus, although autocrats operating in an environment of media suppression have considerably greater latitude to benefit themselves at society's expense, this latitude is not without bounds. In the long run, no government can last that does not have significant support from its citizens and even a hampered underground media can help foment coordinated dissent and rebellion if existing political rulers do not at least minimally satisfy their populations.

Other economists have built on Sen's initial work. Besley and Burgess (2002) provide an empirical test of Sen's hypothesis regarding famine, democracy, and media. Relying on data from the 16 major Indian states, they explore whether governments are more responsive when there is more political competition and a greater number of newspapers. India's 16 states provide an interesting case because there is variation in their vulnerability to famine, as well as in their newspaper circulation and political competition.

Besley and Burgess find that Sen's thesis does in fact hold. A "1 percent increase in newspaper circulation is associated with a 2.4 percent increase in public food distribution and a 5.5 percent increase in calamity relief expenditures" (2002: 1435). Further, they find that the greater the circulation of a newspaper, the greater is the government's response to a crisis. They also find that greater levels of public food distribution are associated with greater political competition. Consistent with Sen's hypothesis, Besley and Burgess conclude their analysis by identifying that "representative democracy and the development of free and independent regional presses appear as key factors in ensuring protection for vulnerable citizens" (2002: 1446).

In a subsequent paper, Besley and Prat (2006) explore how collusion between the government and the media can undermine the effectiveness of media as a check on the behavior of political actors. They conclude that media capture has two major negative effects on the well-being of citizens. First, where the media is captured, the grabbing hand of the state will tend to engage in more rent extraction because political actors are less concerned that they will be "caught" by the public. Second, where government controls the media there will be less political turnover because voters will be unable to punish elected officials due to a lack of information about their ineffectiveness.

While this research focuses on the role of media as a mechanism for monitoring the actions of political actors, a second strand of literature explores the economic implications of various forms of media ownership. Djankov *et al.* (2003) carried out the main research in this area, which asks: Who owns the media? In order to explore this question, the authors develop a dataset on media ownership patterns in 97 countries. The data display two dominant forms of media ownership in the world—state ownership and private ownership in the form of controlling families. The authors use this data to analyze two competing hypotheses regarding media ownership.

The first hypothesis is the public interest, or Pigouvian, theory, which argues that state ownership of the media is desirable because information is a public good that exhibits increasing returns. On the one hand, once information is produced it is costly to exclude people from consuming it. On the other hand, although there are high fixed costs to gathering and distributing information, once these initial costs are covered, the marginal cost of distributing information is extremely low.

The second hypothesis of media ownership is rooted in public choice theory. In contrast to the public interest theory of the media, the public choice view contends that state-owned media will tend to manipulate information to benefit those currently in power. This manipulation will skew reported information in favor of incumbents, which prevents voters from making informed decisions. For this reason, the public choice view concludes that private ownership is preferable to state ownership.

The analysis of Djankov *et al.* supports the public choice view. Specifically, they find that higher levels of state ownership are associated with lower levels of primary school enrollment, lower levels of political rights, and lower levels of civil liberties. Further, countries with higher levels of state ownership of media tend to be poorer and more autocratic, and have higher levels of corruption. These results hold even after controlling for differences in economic development, education, political competition, state intervention in the economy, ethno-linguistic heterogeneity, and latitude.

While the existing literature provides important insights into the connection between media and economic development, it is far from complete. For instance, although it is clear from existing research that media can serve as a check on government, we still lack a full understanding of how media can provide the incentive for officials to adopt policies that are conducive to economic development. Further, while the existing literature discusses the perverse effects of media capture and state ownership of the media, there has been little discussion of how the state actually manipulates media-provided information. Finally, the connection between media and institutional change has yet to be explored. How does media serve as a mechanism that facilitates the process of economic and social change? More specifically, what is the precise channel connecting media, institutional change, and development? Our analysis seeks to fill these gaps.

IS THERE CONSENSUS FOR A FREE AND PRIVATELY-OWNED MEDIA?

While the existing economics literature points to the desirability of privately-owned media, it would be a mistake to conclude that there is a general consensus on this issue. The appearance of consensus that a private and free media is preferable to state ownership overlooks the fact that several arguments exist for government intervention and ownership of the media. These arguments are very much part of the ongoing debate about the desirability of privately-owned media.

For instance, consider the growing media economics literature discussed at the beginning of the previous section. In exploring the economic aspects of information and the structure of the media industry, some of this literature notes how the unregulated market may fail to provide the optimal amount of information (Doyle 2002). The market failures associated with information and media include the public good and externality characteristics of information and the alleged natural monopoly aspects of the media industry. As with market failure stories for other goods and services, the application of this logic to the media market at least in principle leaves room for government intervention to overcome these market failures.

There is an important tension that emerges from these market failure arguments for government intervention in media. As noted above, to the extent that the market for media does suffer from various market failures, there is, at least in theory, some scope for government intervention to serve as a corrective. At the same time, as the literature on media and economic development discussed above indicates, state ownership or regulation of media can lead to many perverse economic outcomes. The question of how much government intervention is desirable in the media industry—if any at all—is therefore still very much open for debate. We will address some of the market failure arguments for government intervention in the media in the concluding chapter.

Traditional political economy, which emphasizes power relations in the economic, political, and social spheres, has also produced a large literature analyzing the media (see for instance, Herman and Chomsky 1988; Bagdikian 1990; Golding and Murdock 1997). This literature tends to be skeptical of media that emerges on the free market. This pessimism stems from the view that two main groups of capitalists—media owners and advertisers—will use media as a tool of manipulating the masses. Those writing in this tradition argue that the media that emerges in a capitalistic system fails to provide a diversity of information, perspectives, and cultural resources to the public.

Solutions to these perceived problems vary widely. Some argue that despite its problems, a private media is still preferable given the alternatives. Others call on the state to play an active role in the media industry. There is again no consensus about the desirable extent of government intervention in the media market, with proposals ranging from government regulation of private media, to subsidies to certain media outlets, to outright state ownership of at least part of the media.

Similar to the media economics literature that emphasizes market failure, the traditional political economy literature also highlights the fact that agreement about the desirability of a free media characterized by private ownership is far from reached. As such, sharpening our understanding of the way media influences economic development, as well as how different ownership structures influence the effectiveness of media in this regard, is critically important.

THE IMPORTANCE OF POLICIES AND INSTITUTIONS FOR ECONOMIC DEVELOPMENT

Our main focus in this book is on the role of media in economic develop-ment. Both policies and institutions matter for economic outcomes and we will focus on both throughout this book. Given this, it is important to distinguish between policies and institutions and to clarify the connec-tion between institutions and economic development. Institutions can be understood as the formal and informal rules governing human behavior, and the enforcement of these rules (North 1990). Formal institutions include codified institutions that are intentionally designed. Examples would include state-made constitutions, legislation, and formal standards. In contrast, informal institutions evolve over time and are not the result of intentional design. They include, for example, norms, conventions, and what is generally referred to as culture.

Institutions differ from policies in that the former are typically durable and stable over time while the latter can and do change more frequently. The overarching "meta-rules" and structures of a political system would be an example of institutions. The various political choice variables, such as tax rates, spending decisions, and so on, made within, and emerging from, those institutions, would be examples of policies. Both policies and institutions influence economic development or the lack thereof. As we will discuss throughout this book, the media can play an important role in influencing and reinforcing both institutions *and* policies.

The enforcement of both formal and informal institutions can occur through the internalization of certain norms of behavior, the social pres-sure exerted on the individual by the group, or the power of third-party enforcers who threaten to use force against individuals who violate rules. Institutions reduce uncertainty by providing a predictable structure in which people can act. In providing the rules of the game, institutions shape economic, social, and political interactions. As such, differences in economic outcomes across societies and countries can be attributed to different institutional structures (see Olson 1996). Moreover, changes in institutions, for better or worse, directly influence changes in economic well-being.

Nobel Laureate economist Douglass North (1990) is best known for developing a theory of institutions, as well as analyzing the evolution of institutions and the consequences of those institutions for economic per-formance. Building on North's initial work in this area, a growing number of empirical studies analyze the importance of institutions for economic outcomes. These studies analyze institutional explanations for economic development and compare them with other potential explanations, such as geography, fractionalization, and trade integration.

The most well-known recent empirical work that examines the impact of institutions on economic performance is a series of articles by Acemoglu, Johnson and Robinson (2001, 2002). These authors explore the effect of institutions on income in ex-colonies. Some of these countries, such as the United States, New Zealand, and Australia, exhibit high levels of economic development. Others, such as the majority of countries in Sub-Saharan Africa, display the reverse.

The authors argue that this variation in income across the ex-colonies can be explained by the property rights institutions these countries developed as a result of the different kinds of disease environments that colonizers faced. According to their analysis, the property rights institutions we observe across these countries today were determined by the property rights institutions they inherited from their colonizers. In places like the United States, New Zealand, and Australia, the prevalence of diseases such as malaria at the time of colonization was relatively low. Thus, colonizers could settle in these places in large numbers with the intention of staying for a long time. Since, as inhabitants of these countries, colonizers would be subject to the long-run effects of the property rights institutions they created, where they settled more permanently it was in their interest to establish institutions of long-run economic growth, namely well-protected private property rights.

In contrast, in other countries, such as those in Sub-Saharan Africa, diseases like malaria were rampant and posed a serious threat to the lives of colonizers. In these places, colonizers could not settle permanently. This shaped their colonizing strategy in that it created a very short-run time horizon for the colonizers. They sought to get in, extract as many resources as possible, and get out. This led colonizers in these places to establish extractive institutions that poorly protected citizens' private property rights.

The key finding of Acemoglu, Johnson and Robinson's study is that private property rights are the primary determinant of nations' levels of economic development. This is true even after controlling for other potential determinants of income, such as colonizer identity (for example, British or French), and a variety of geographic variables like latitude, distance from a coast, and climate, which some have argued are responsible for the wealth and poverty of nations (see for instance, Gallup, Sachs and Mellinger 1999; Sachs 2001, 2003).

Building on this work, Acemoglu and Johnson (2005) have gone further in clarifying the type of property institutions that are important for economic development. They point to the fact that there are multiple types of

property-protecting institutions that may matter for economic development. On the one hand there are what they call "contracting institutions,"
such as government courts, that enforce private agreements between
citizens. These institutions are important because they aim to protect the
property rights of citizens vis-à-vis one another. On the other hand there
are "property rights institutions," such as constraints on the government's
ability to seize citizens' property arbitrarily. These institutions are important because they aim to protect the private property rights of citizens
against government predation.

Acemoglu and Johnson's work aims to "unbundle" these two private
property-related institutions to see which is more important for economic
development. Alternatively, their analysis can be thought of as asking
which type of predation—public or private—poses the greater threat to
economic development. The conclusion of this study is that "property
rights institutions"—institutions that restrain government expropriation—
are substantially more important than "contracting institutions"—state-
provided institutions to prevent private predation—for nearly all aspects
of economic development. State expropriation, not predation by private
individuals, is more harmful to economic progress, and thus more important to prevent. Conversely, institutional restraints that prevent government from violating the private property rights of their citizens are the
dominant determinant of economic development.

Other empirical research also supports the importance of property
rights institutions for economic development. For instance, Rodrik,
Subramanian and Trebbi (2004) analyze three possible explanations—
geography, trade integration, and institutions—for differences in income
across countries. They conclude that the quality of institutions is the most
important factor in explaining differences in income. After controlling for
institutions, the authors of this study find that geography has a weak direct
effect on income while trade integration has no direct effect. The findings
of this work further support the original empirical research by Acemoglu,
Johnson and Robinson (2001, 2002) in this area concerning the primacy of
institutions for economic development. Given the importance of institutions in contributing to economic performance, our analysis focuses on the
role media plays in supporting or undermining an institutional structure
conducive to development.

THE PROCESS OF INSTITUTIONAL CHANGE

While the aforementioned literature emphasizes the importance of
institutions for economic development, much less is known about the

process of institutional change. Given the importance of institutions for economic performance, how do quality institutions emerge where they do not already exist? How do countries currently characterized by poor-quality institutions turn the corner toward economic progress and development?

Institutions that exist in the current period are the result of past choices and experiences (North 1990; David 1994; Boettke, Coyne and Leeson 2008). A growing economics literature focusing on institutional "path dependency" emphasizes that the way institutions and beliefs developed in past periods constrains the set of feasible choices in the current period (North 1990: 93–98, 2005: 51–52). Denzau and North (1994) and North (2005) place informal institutions, and especially "belief systems," at the core of the process of institutional change.[2] North (2005: 23) notes that "the process works as follows: the beliefs that humans hold determine the choices they make that, in turn, structure the changes in the human landscape." This indicates that if we wish to understand institutional differences and institutional change, we must start with the "mental models" or belief systems guiding individual actions.

In this context, institutional change entails shifts in fundamental belief systems. As Denzau and North (1994) and North (2005) make clear, individuals rely on an incomplete mental model since they cannot know the full range of possible opportunities that currently exist or will exist in the future. As individuals become aware of alternative courses of actions they incorporate those possibilities into their mental models. When new alternatives are introduced, or the relative prices of existing alternatives change, mental models are updated and institutions evolve.

Institutional change is typically gradual and slow. This results in marginal changes to existing institutions as individuals update their mental models and belief systems. However, when mental models and perceptions change drastically, the result can be dramatic institutional change resulting in a new "punctuated" institutional equilibrium. The process of punctuated institutional change involves long periods of slow institutional change punctuated by short periods of significant institutional change characterized by "periods of representational redescription" (Denzau and North 1994: 23). In contrast to gradual changes, which are marginal in nature, punctuated changes represent significant changes in the nature of institutions. The collapse of communism, which few were able to accurately predict, is one example of this logic.

How does a punctuated equilibrium emerge? The process that creates punctuated institutional change begins with a divergence between underlying beliefs and the status quo, or what Denzau and North call the growing gap "between the general climate of opinion and the 'pure' ideology"

(1994: 25). Timur Kuran's discussion (1995) of "preference falsification"—when individuals publicly lie about their private preferences—highlights this divergence.

As Kuran point out, once a minimum threshold of people holding certain private preferences is met, even a minor event can lead to dramatic changes in economic, social, and political institutions. One example of this is political revolutions. Central to such revolutions is the activation of "tipping points" for punctuated institutional change. Once the growing gap between actual and public preferences reaches some threshold, a tipping point may be activated making major institutional change possible. After the tipping point is activated and the new punctuated institutional equilibrium is established, the process of slow and gradual change that Denzau and North (1994) emphasize re-emerges, restarting the process described above.

Understanding the process of institutional change thus entails identifying mechanisms that can change the fundamental belief systems of the members of a society. We argue that media is one such mechanism. Given its potential to reach a large number of consumers, the media has the ability to change fundamental belief systems by making individuals aware of alternative courses of action. As such, the media has the ability to generate changes in perceptions and mental models which may lead to both gradual changes to existing institutions and more dramatic punctuated institutional changes.

The story of the role of media in the downfall of Vladimiro Montesinos that opened this chapter illustrates many of media's characteristics in this regard. In this case, media provided information that allowed individuals to update their belief systems. It also produced common knowledge so that citizens were confident that others were updating their mental models as well. This allowed for widespread coordination around institutional change resulting in the downfall of the ruling regime.

It is important to note that the evolution of belief systems is endogenous and takes place within an existing structure of formal and informal institutions. This existing structure will influence and constrain the evolution of institutions. In order for formal institutions to operate effectively, they must be supported by informal institutions. However, formal institutions—whether supported by informal institutions or not—will influence the evolution of informal institutions.

While informal institutions constrain the effectiveness of formal institutions, existing formal institutions simultaneously influence and constrain the evolution of informal institutions. They do so by establishing and enforcing the formal rules through which individuals are exposed to alternative beliefs and possibilities. To understand this point, consider that dictators expend a great deal of resources controlling the media and dissemination of information in their countries. Their aim is to restrict citizens' awareness of alternative institutional possibilities. If a dictator prevents those living under him from being exposed to alternative forms of economic, political, and social organization, citizens are unable to incorporate those alternatives into their belief systems. Because of this, the evolution of informal institutions, and hence formal institutions, is curtailed.

THE DUAL ROLE OF MEDIA

In both the theoretical and applied analysis of media that follows, we emphasize the dual role of media. First, the media can influence policies within given institutions. Amartya Sen's work, which focuses on the media as a disciplinary device, captures this aspect. For citizens to effectively discipline officials, they must have access to accurate information regarding their actions. The media can increase transparency regarding the actions of officials. In doing so, it reduces the cost of information accumulation facing citizens. As a result, citizens are better informed regarding the behaviors and policies adopted by those who rule them. To the extent that the media is effective in this regard, there will be pressure on officials to consider citizens' welfare in deciding policy.

Second, the media can serve as a catalyst of gradual and dramatic institutional change, and as a mechanism for reinforcing those changes once they take place. As noted above, the process of institutional change involves changes in mental models and belief systems. In presenting alternative information, ideas, and perceptions, the media can serve as a mechanism of institutional change. As we point out above, typically, institutional change is slow and gradual. In other words, changes in mental models and belief systems lead to marginal changes in existing institutions. However, we also observe dramatic "punctuated" changes in existing institutions. These dramatic changes involve significant alterations in the very constitution of institutions. As our case studies discuss, media can play an important role in bringing about both gradual and dramatic changes in institutions. Further, once dramatic institutional change takes place, media can play an important role in reinforcing the punctuated institutional equilibrium. In this regard, the media creates continuing consensus around new institutions, contributing to their durability over time.

Note that these two roles are not mutually exclusive and can influence one another. For example, institutional change will influence the feasible set of policies through changes in incentives facing policymakers. Likewise, policies adopted can reinforce or erode existing institutions.

THREE EFFECTS OF MEDIA ON INSTITUTIONS AND INSTITUTIONAL CHANGE

Media can be both a catalyst of institutional change, as well as a means of reinforcing changes once they take place. We identify three specific effects of media on policies and institutions (see Coyne and Leeson 2009):

1. *Gradual effect*   The "gradual effect" of media refers to its ability to introduce marginal changes by slowly influencing consumers' ideas, perceptions, and information. Since individuals typically update their mental models slowly, the process of institutional change is often gradual. Media can facilitate this gradual change by presenting individuals with information for new mental models—ideas and perceptions that differ from the status quo. As individuals' mental models gradually change, the gap between their desires and existing institutions gradually grows as well, creating pressure for small institutional change. Gradual changes are reflected through citizens' demand for changes in policy or existing institutions. These changes are marginal, meaning that they do not change the fundamental nature or constitution of existing institutions.

2. *Punctuation effect*   This refers to media's ability to facilitate major institutional change. In this role, mass media activates potential tipping points, assisting dramatic institutional change. This in turn influences the set of feasible policies which can be adopted. The process works as follows. If the divergence between private and public preference becomes significant, opportunity for punctuated institutional change—rapid and dramatic institutional overhaul—emerges.

    Not all opportunities for punctuated changes lead to actual changes, however. The reason is that dispersed and anonymous individuals cannot always coordinate their beliefs and actions, activating the tipping point required for a punctuation possibility to become reality. For example, opportunities for punctuated change may go unrealized if individuals do not know that others share similar private preferences for change. Here, individuals' preference for change remains private, preventing the coordination required to seize an opportunity. A "preference gap" that satisfies some minimum threshold is therefore necessary but not sufficient for punctuated institutional change. To be sufficient, society must take advantage of reaching this threshold by activating tipping points—converting opportunity for punctuated institutional change into actual punctuated institutional change—which requires a solution to a "coordination problem." The media can serve as a coordination mechanism, converting potential tipping points into actual punctuated changes.

3. *Reinforcement effect* This refers to media's ability to reinforce existing punctuated equilibria once they are established. The same capacity of media to generate common knowledge to create change, as in the gradual and punctuated effects, can also reinforce existing institutions. Media can do this by creating common knowledge that supports existing policies and institutions instead of common knowledge that encourages new ones. For example, if a recent punctuated institutional change displaced illiberal institutions with liberal ones and these institutions are working well, this success may be broadcast with individuals' support for the new regime, improving individuals' knowledge that others also view the new institutions favorably, reinforcing the new arrangement.

In the analysis that follows, we place particular emphasis on the various factors that influence these three effects of media on policies and institutions. We emphasize that while a free media is the "first best," even a relatively unfree media can have an important impact on changes in policies and institutions for the better.

In addition to understanding the role of media in policy and institutional change, and hence economic development, our analysis helps to resolve an important tension in the literature on institutions and institutional change. On the one hand, we know institutions change—sometimes dramatically and rapidly. On the other hand, a central characteristic of institutions is their durability. How do we reconcile observed institutional changes with institutional durability? We identify mass media's varying effects, described above, as a specific mechanism that explains institutional change and durability. The media serves as a catalyst of gradual and dramatic change as well as a means of reinforcing existing policies and institutions.

THE OUTLINE OF THIS BOOK

Our examination of media's role in economic development is broad and consists of theoretical, qualitative, and quantitative analysis. Combining these various approaches and methods provides different perspectives on the problem at hand and hence a more complete understanding of our topic of study.

In the next chapter we develop "The Reformers' Dilemma," a theoretical model of the process of policy and institutional change. Drawing on some basic concepts from game theory, we clarify the fundamental dilemma facing policymakers in developing countries. We also model the process of citizen coordination around new conjectures and belief systems. We argue that media can be a coordination-enhancing mechanism around both changes in policy within institutions, as well as gradual and dramatic changes in institutions. We also highlight how media can reinforce changes once they have taken place.

Chapter 3 explores several key factors influencing the dual role and the three effects of media discussed above. The first factor is government intervention in the media. As discussed earlier, much of the existing literature on media and economic development has focused either on media as a check on government or on various media ownership patterns. This literature highlights some of the costs and perverse economic outcomes associated with government ownership of media. We contribute to this discussion by identifying the specific ways government manipulates the media and weakens its effectiveness as both a check on government and as a mechanism of change.

We then turn to an analysis of how the legal environment impacts media freedom. Our focus here is on information transparency and the protection of journalists and media employees from direct and indirect coercion. Media quality is the next factor we consider. We focus on the importance of journalists' standards and ethics for delivering accurate and timely information to consumers. Finally, we consider the economic factors that influence media. We focus on consumer demand and the importance of a private advertising sector for sustainable media independence. Our contention is that a free media plays an important role in the broader process of economic development. Although even where it is unfree the media can have an important effect on social change, a free media is a first-best situation because it is most effective in fully exploiting media's ability to enhance economic development. However, while a free media is necessary for economic development, it is not, by itself, sufficient. Relevant information must be available to media outlets and that information must be reported accurately and ethically. Finally, consumers must demand certain types of information in order for media to be effective in contributing to economic development.

The next two chapters provide both empirical and qualitative analysis. Utilizing data regarding Eastern and Central Europeans' political knowledge, Chapter 4 statistically analyzes the relationship between media freedom and citizens' political knowledge. Focusing on an environment of democratic political competition, this analysis explores the connection between state ownership of media, political knowledge, political participation, and voter turnout. The main finding is that in countries where government has greater control over the media, citizens are more politically ignorant and apathetic. Chapter 5 complements this empirical analysis by presenting three case studies focusing on media's role in policy and institutional change, as well as in the broader process of economic development. While the statistical evidence in Chapter 4 establishes general patterns, these case studies allow us to trace the causal mechanisms in more detail while paying particular attention to the specific context in which media outlets operate and evolve. These two chapters illustrate the analysis provided in previous chapters.

In the final chapter we conclude by discussing the implications of our analysis. In addition to discussing the implications of media for economic development, we provide some clear policy steps regarding the movement toward a free media in developing countries. Because a media free from government manipulation and control is a first-best outcome, we focus on providing a policy blueprint for achieving this end. In doing so, we also address some of the concerns regarding "market failures" in media and information markets in developing countries.

NOTES

1. This is not to dismiss the issue of bias but rather to highlight that in many countries the central media issue is one of the extent and magnitude of state involvement in the media. For an economic analysis of media-driven biases, see Sutter (2004). Mullainathan and Shleifer (2005), and Gentzkow and Shapiro (2006) examine market-driven news biases.
2. Others exploring the process of institutional change include David (1994), Greif (1994), Young (1998), Aoki (2001, 2007), Greif and Laitin (2004).

REFERENCES

Acemoglu, Daron and Simon Johnson (2005) "Unbundling Institutions," *Journal of Political Economy*, 115: 949–995.

Acemoglu, Daron, Simon Johnson, and James Robinson (2001) "The Colonial Origins of Comparative Development: An Empirical Investigation," *American Economic Review*, 91: 1369–1401.

Acemoglu, Daron, Simon Johnson, and James Robinson (2002) "Reversal of Fortunes: Geography and Institutions in the Making of the Modern World Income Distribution," *Quarterly Journal of Economics*, 117: 1231–1294.

Albarran, Alan B. (2002) *Media Economics: Understanding Markets, Industries and Concepts*. Iowa City, IA: Iowa State Press.

Aoki, Masahiko (2001) *Toward a Comparative Institutional Analysis*. Cambridge, MA: MIT Press.

Aoki, Masahiko (2007) "Endogenizing Institutions and Institutional Changes," *Journal of Institutional Economics*, 3(1): 1–31.

Bagdikian, Ben H. (1990) *The Media Monopoly*. Boston, MA: Beacon.
Bartels, Larry (1993) "Messages Received: The Political Impact of Media Exposure," *American Political Science Review*, 87: 267–285.
Besley, Timothy and Robin Burgess (2002) "The Political Economy of Government Responsiveness: Theory and Evidence from India," *Quarterly Journal of Economics*, 117: 1415–1452.
Besley, Timothy and Andrea Prat (2006) "Handcuffs for the Grabbing Hand? Media Capture and Government Accountability," *American Economic Review*, 96: 720–736.
Boettke, Peter J., Christopher J. Coyne and Peter T. Leeson (2008) "Institutional Stickiness and the New Development Economics," *American Journal of Economics and Sociology*, 67: 331–358.
Bowen, Sally and Jane Holligan (2003) *The Imperfect Spy: The Many Worlds of Vladimiro Montesinos*. Lima: Peisa.
Brians, Craig Leonard and Martin P. Wattenberg (1996) "Campaign Issue Knowledge and Salience: Comparing Reception from TV Commercials, TV News and Newspapers," *American Journal of Political Science*, XL: 172–193.
Coyne, Christopher J. and Peter T. Leeson (2009) "Media as a Mechanism of Institutional Change and Reinforcement,' *Kyklos*, 62(1): 1–14.
David, Paul (1994) "Why Are Institutions the 'Carriers of History': Path-Dependence and the Evolution of Conventions, Organizations and Institutions," *Structural Change and Economic Dynamics*, 5(2): 205–220.
Denzau, Arthur and Douglass C. North (1994) "Shared Mental Models: Ideologies and Institutions," *Kyklos*, 47: 3–31.
Djankov, Simeon, Caralee McLiesh, Tatiana Nenova, and Andrei Shleifer (2003) "Who Owns the Media?" *Journal of Law and Economics*, 46: 341–382.
Doyle, Gillian (2002). *Understanding Media Economics*. Thousand Oaks, CA: Sage Publications Ltd.
Freedom House (2008) *Freedom of the Press 2008: A Global Survey of Media Independence*. New York: Rowman and Littlefield.
Gallup, John, Jeffrey Sachs, and Andrew Mellinger (1999) "Geography and Economic Development," *International Regional Science Review*, 22: 179–232.
Gentzkow, Matthew and Jesse Shapiro (2006) "Media Bias and Reputation," *Journal of Political Economy*, 114(2): 280–316.
Goldberg, Bernard (2003) *Bias: A CBS Insider Exposes How the Media Distort the News*. New York: Harper Paperbacks.
Golding, Peter and Graham Murdock (eds) (1997) *The Political Economy of the Media*, 2 volumes. Cheltenham, UK: Edward Elgar Publishing Limited.
Greif, Avner (1994) "Cultural Beliefs and the Organization of Society: Historical and Theoretical Reflection on Collectivist and Individualist Societies," *Journal of Political Economy*, 102(5): 912–950.
Greif, Avner and David D. Laitin (2004) "A Theory of Endogenous Institutional Change," *American Political Science Review*, 98: 633–652.
Hardin, Russell (1999) *Liberalism, Constitutionalism, and Democracy*. New York: Oxford University Press.
Herman, E. and Noam Chomsky (1988) *Manufacturing Consent*. New York: Pantheon.
Kuran, Timur (1995) *Private Truths, Public Lies: The Social Consequences of Preference Falsification*. Cambridge, MA: Harvard University Press.

Kuypers, Jim A. (2002) *Press Bias and Politics: How the Media Frame Controversial Issues*. Westport, CT: Praeger Publishers.

McMillan, John and Pablo Zoido (2004) "How to Subvert Democracy: Montesinos in Peru," *The Journal of Economic Perspectives* 18(4): 69–92.

Mondak, Jeffrey J. (1995) "Newspapers and Political Awareness," *American Journal of Political Science*, XXXIX: 513–527.

Mullainathan, Sendhil and Andrei Shleifer (2005) "The Market for News," *American Economic Review*, 95(4): 1031–1053.

North, Douglass C. (1990) *Institutions, Institutional Change and Economic Performance*. Cambridge: Cambridge University Press.

North, Douglass C. (2005) *Understanding the Process of Economic Change*. Princeton, NJ: Princeton University Press.

Olson, Mancur (1996) "Big Bills Left on the Sidewalk: Why Some Nations are Rich and Others are Poor," *Journal of Economic Perspectives*, 10(2): 3–24.

Rodrik, Dani, Arvind Subramanian and Francesco Trebbi (2004) "Institutions Rule: The Primacy of Institutions Over Geography and Integration in Economic Development," *Journal of Economic Growth*, 9: 131–165.

Sachs, Jeffrey (2001) *Topical Underdevelopment*, NBER Working Paper No. 8119. Cambridge, MA: NBER.

Sachs, Jeffrey (2003) *Institutions Don't Rule: Direct Effects of Geography on Per Capita Income*, NBER Working Paper No. 9490. Cambridge, MA: NBER.

Sen, Amartya (1984) *Poverty and Famines*. Oxford: Oxford University Press.

Sen, Amartya (1999) *Development as Freedom*. New York: Alfred A. Knopf Inc.

Sutter, Daniel (2004) "News Media Incentives, Coverage of Government and the Growth of Government," *Independent Review*, 8(4): 549–567.

Weingast, Barry R. (1995) "The Economic Role of Political Institutions: Market-Preserving Federalism and Economic Development," *Journal of Law, Economics and Organization*, 11(1): 1–31.

Weingast, Barry R. (1997) "The Political Foundations of Democracy and the Rule of Law," *American Political Science Review*, 91(2): 245–263.

World Bank (2002) *The World Development Report 2002: Building Institutions for Markets*. New York: Oxford University Press, Inc.

Young, H. Peyton (1998) *Individual Strategy and Social Structure: An Evolutionary Theory of Institutions*. Princeton, NJ: Princeton University Press.

2. The Reformers' Dilemma

INTRODUCTION

To analyze the role of media in economic development, we need to first understand the fundamental dilemma facing reformers. The policies and institutions required for economic development are well known. Writing over 250 years ago, Adam Smith noted that "Little else is requisite to carry a state to the highest degree of opulence from the lowest barbarism, but peace, easy taxes, and a tolerable administration of justice; all the rest being brought about by the natural course of things" (1775: xliii). More recently, Dani Rodrik (2007: 21), echoing Smith, has noted that "A semblance of property rights, sound money, fiscal solvency, market-oriented incentives—these are elements common to all successful growth strategies." Subsequent empirical research has supported Smith's claim regarding the importance of economic freedom (that is, low barriers to entry and exit and minimal regulation and taxes), private property and the rule of law for economic progress (see for instance Scully 1988; Hanke and Walters 1997; Gwartney *et al.* 1999).

Despite social scientists' understanding of what economic development requires, we have a poor understanding of how to establish these policies and institutions where they do not already exist. Why do institutions conducive to economic development emerge in some countries but not others? Further, why do policymakers in some countries adopt policies that generate economic growth while others fail to do so?

To explore these questions we develop a theoretical model that illuminates the fundamental dilemma facing reformers. Our model draws on some basic concepts from game theory to provide a means of formally analyzing the strategic interaction between the players involved in the reform process—that is, the process of policy and institutional change that works toward Adam Smith's recipe for development. Moreover, our model serves to clarify media's role in the process of economic development and institutional change.

THE REFORMERS' DILEMMA: WHY POLITICIANS DO NOT ADOPT POLICY AND INSTITUTIONAL REFORMS

Our model is based on the work of Nobel Laureate economist Thomas Schelling (1960), who emphasized the difference between games of conflict and games of cooperation. Social and political interactions can be classified along a spectrum with games of pure conflict on one end, games of pure cooperation on the other, and many combinations of mixed coordination/conflict games in between. Within this context, we begin with the classic Prisoners' Dilemma illustrated in Figure 2.1. This game lies on the pure conflict end of the spectrum and is the standard starting point for the analysis of conflict and cooperation in economic, social, and political interactions.

The left-hand payoff in each cell represents Player 1's payoff and the right-hand payoff represents Player 2's payoff. When both players cooperate, they both receive α. If one agent attempts to cooperate while the other defects, the cooperating agent receives θ, while the defecting agent receives γ. If each agent defects, they each earn only β. In the game illustrated in Figure 2.1, $\gamma > \alpha > \beta > \theta$ where $2\alpha > (\gamma + \theta) > 2\beta$, which is to say that mutual cooperation is socially efficient. However, the Nash equilibrium of the one-shot version of this game is for both individuals to

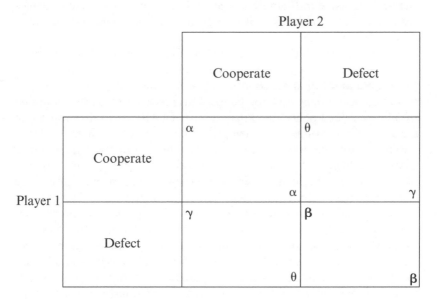

Figure 2.1   The Prisoners' Dilemma—a situation of pure conflict

defect, as illustrated by the emboldened lower right-hand cell. No matter what strategy the one player chooses, the other player will always secure a greater payoff by choosing to defect. Since the payoff to each individual player from choosing to defect is higher than that associated with cooperating, both players defect. However, when both players defect, the collective outcome is worse than if they had cooperated. The Prisoners' Dilemma illustrates a situation where a conflict of interests exists between two players and shows that when both people in the game pursue their individual private interest, they do not promote the collective interest of the group.

The process of policy and institutional reform in developing countries fits the Prisoners' Dilemma scenario well. The players in this context are policymakers and the strategies they are considering include adopting policy and institutional reforms consistent with Smith's basic recipe for economic growth or engaging in activities that cut against Smith's recipe, such as catering to special interest groups at the expense of social welfare. The former strategy corresponds to the cooperative strategy in Figure 2.1. The latter strategy constitutes the defection strategy in this figure.

The policymakers in this game should be understood in the broadest sense as any political actors with a say in the policies and institutions governing a particular region or country. Although the particular form of government these policymakers exist in will influence the particulars of the "game," the game in Figure 2.1 is general and applies as much to democratically elected politicos as it does to political actors under autocratic government.

To see why it is in the private interest of each policymaker to cater to special interests even when the other does not, consider the following. In the absence of binding, coordination-enhancing rules to the contrary, there is a strong incentive for political agents to refrain from adopting socially beneficial policies and institutions. This is due to the presence of special interest groups that attempt to influence policy. Special interest groups are formed because they allow members to pursue their political goals with increased efficiency through specialization and the division of labor. Due to these increased efficiencies, special interest groups are effectively able to concentrate benefits on their members while dispersing the costs associated with these benefits among tax-paying citizens who are non-members. The specifics of interest groups vary widely from country to country. In some cases interest groups may represent specific industries and in others they represent family and friends that receive special treatment from the ruling elite. We use the term in the broadest sense to refer to those groups that seek their own narrow interest at the expense of the broader social welfare.

Policymakers that successfully cater to special interest groups benefit the members of these groups and themselves. Under democratic forms of government they might benefit themselves by securing votes, campaign contributions, or other forms of "political currency." In non-democratic systems, policymakers may strengthen their positions of power by catering to military leaders, cronies, or other pockets of the population important for supporting and enabling their rule. Catering to special interest groups therefore benefits the policymaker who does so at the expense of competing policymakers regardless of the political system involved. If only one policymaker caters to special interest groups, he[1] is able to successfully out-compete his rival because of the greater political currency he enjoys by doing so. To prevent this situation, both policymakers therefore have an incentive to cater to special interest groups to secure a competitive position vis-à-vis the other.

This is potentially problematic from the perspective of social welfare on two fronts. First, even if both policymakers would prefer to undertake growth-enhancing reforms instead of catering to special interest groups, neither is able to do so. This is because either policymaker can "oust" the other by catering to special interest groups, enlarging their political currency and therefore "defeating" the other with greater support from the interest groups that form the political support base for their position of power. This "ousting" can be literal if the policymakers are part of a democratic political regime, in which case the policymaker who caters to special interest groups defeats the one who does not at the voting booth. Or this "ousting" can refer to a policymaker's power being diminished or eliminated among those in the monopoly ruling party in an autocratic regime.

Second, and perhaps even more importantly, catering to special interest groups is costly to citizens' welfare. As Mancur Olson (1982) has demonstrated, the short-run gains of special interest groups can have devastating long-run effects on a society in terms of economic stagnation and decline. As such, establishing institutional rules to limit the influence of special interests is of the utmost important for the long-run economic health of a society. Stated differently, mechanisms must be put in place to provide political agents with the incentive to adopt policies and respect institutions that contribute to the general welfare instead of catering to narrow interests. As we will discuss shortly, the media is one such mechanism.

In this way, catering to special interest groups instead of adopting pro-growth economic reform is potentially damaging to two sets of interests. On the one hand, even policymakers devoted to genuine reform will find it difficult to achieve their desired goal. On the other hand, because the policymakers' dominant strategy is to cater to special interest groups, society suffers.

Political Agent 1

		Adopt Reform	Cater to Special Interests
Political Agent 2	Adopt Reform	(a, a) X	$(0, b)$ Y
	Cater to Special Interests	$(b, 0)$ Y	**$(b/2, b/2)$** Y

Figure 2.2   The Reformers' Dilemma

Given these insights, we model the reform process as a modified Prisoners' Dilemma situation. This framework captures the essential features of interaction between political agents. In our framework there are two key players, political agents, who may either "adopt reform"—that is, undertake socially beneficial policy or institutional reform—or cater to special interest groups. Although this game only has two players, it reflects three sets of interests: the interests of political agent 1, political agent 2, and the citizens.[2] Figure 2.2 depicts this game, which we call the Reformers' Dilemma.[3]

The private payoffs to political agents are in the upper left-hand corner of each box and are a, b, $b/2$ and 0, where $b > a > b/2 > 0$. The lower right-hand corner of each box contains the payoffs to society in each case, X and Y, where $X > Y$. When both agents adopt a policy or institutional reform beneficial to economic development, both receive some payoff, a, in the form of revenue generated from taxing a high level of social wealth. In this case social wealth is maximized and society's payoff is X. However, this revenue is less than each agent could receive by catering to special interest groups when the other agent does not, b. When only one agent caters to special interest groups this agent receives all the gains from catering while the other receives zero. Because reform is tailored to special interests rather than maximizing social wealth, the public receives a lower payoff, Y.

When both agents cater to special interests, each receives gains, but the total gains are divided and each agent receives a payoff of only $b/2$. At any given point in time the number of rents available for "offering" by politicians to special interests is fixed. The same "amount" of special interest catering thus occurs whether one or both agents engage in the practice. So, although the spoils are distributed differently, the negative effect on social wealth caused by catering to special interests instead of adopting beneficial policies is the same in either case, leading again to a public payoff of Y.

To clarify this last point further, consider the following example. Social wealth is damaged equally if one political agent caters to special interests by subsidizing two farmers in the amount of $1 million each and the other subsidizes no one, or if one political agent subsidizes one farmer for $1 million and the other political agent subsidizes the other farmer for $1 million. Although the political agents' individual payoffs are different in each case—in the first case (2, 0) and in the second case (1, 1)—the net cost to society is $2 million in both events.

As Figure 2.2 illustrates, similar to the logic in the basic Prisoners' Dilemma in Figure 2.1, political agents' dominant strategy is to cater to special interests. This equilibrium is not only suboptimal for the political agents, but for society as well. Both political agents and citizens in general would be made better off by moving to the "adopt reform–adopt reform" equilibrium. As such, success in the reform process requires finding a solution to the Reformers' Dilemma that provides an incentive for policymakers to forgo the private benefits of catering to special interests and instead adopt socially beneficial policy and institutional reforms.

OVERCOMING THE REFORMERS' DILEMMA

The real-world Reformers' Dilemma does not correspond precisely to the strictures required in the game-theoretic model put forth above (see Tullock 1999). In reality, play may be repeated, players may select their partners, and players can communicate. The absence of these features makes the game-theoretic dilemma insurmountable. But in the real world, it is precisely through these avenues that we can find a solution to the Reformers' Dilemma. The potential for repeated dealings, the threat of punishment for defection, and communication regarding punishment allows for the possibility of a cooperative outcome.

In order to better understand this point, consider the folk theorem. This suggests that a multi-period Prisoners' Dilemma may have a cooperative solution, provided that: 1) individuals are sufficiently patient, 2) there are low information-sharing costs, and 3) agents have a common and shared idea about "defection" and how it should be punished. If these conditions hold, cooperation can be an equilibrium. Those who fail to cooperate will receive a short-term benefit but will also receive many future periods of punishment. Further, the repercussions for defection will be common knowledge among the players involved. Once in place, these conditions

Media, development, and institutional change

Political Agents 1 and 2

		Good Conjectures	Bad Conjectures
Populace	Good Conjectures	φ φ	---
	Bad Conjectures	--- 	σ σ

Figure 2.3   The Coordination Game—a situation of pure cooperation

will be mutually reinforcing and generate a binding rule that facilitates and enforces cooperation.

Assuming that the conditions for cooperation according to the folk theorem hold, the game of conflict reflected in the Reformers' Dilemma in Figure 2.2 can be transformed into the multi-person coordination game depicted in Figure 2.3. "Good Conjectures" refer to beliefs and expectations that support socially beneficial policies and institutions that generate economic development. For example, if political agents and the populace are dedicated to a balanced budget, liberal trade policy, and market-driven business activity, they will have coordinated on good conjectures—that is, conjectures that facilitate economic progress. Likewise, coordination around institutions respecting existing property rights would lead to economic development, as noted by Adam Smith long ago.

In contrast, "Bad Conjectures" refer to beliefs and expectations that contribute to economic stagnation. For instance, if political agents and citizens commit to deficit spending, protectionist trade policy, and state subsidization of failing businesses, they will have coordinated on bad conjectures—that is, conjectures that retard economic development. Similarly, coordination around institutions that fail to respect private property or provide constraints on the power of policymakers will lead to negative economic outcomes.

As Figure 2.3 illustrates, coordination of effort premised upon good conjectures yields positive payoffs to all parties, as illustrated by the upper-left corner payoff. It is also possible, however, that individuals may coordinate efforts premised upon bad conjectures, which yield lower payoffs, as illustrated by the lower-right corner. In this game, $\varphi > \sigma$ and both players prefer the good conjecture equilibrium in which they earn the higher payoff (φ, φ) to the bad conjecture equilibrium in which they earn the lower payoff (σ, σ).

The higher payoff of coordination on good conjectures reflects the greater long-run wealth that flows from dedication to growth-enhancing policies. If all players know the payoffs of this game, which is to say that this game is one of complete information, coordination on good conjectures will occur. Whether such payoffs are in fact common knowledge, however, or if instead a situation of incomplete information leads to coordination on bad conjectures, is an issue we will return to later when we discuss citizens' demands for certain types of media-provided information.

The game in Figure 2.3 captures the fact that securing cooperation between political agents is not enough to achieve economic development. The populace must demand and support the policies and institutions for them to be implemented and effective. Assuming that political actors agree to adopt a policy or institutional change, they must coordinate with the population on healthy and constructive conjectures that yield the higher payoffs illustrated by the upper-left box. However, it is also possible that the populace and politicians may coordinate on bad conjectures, which yield lower payoffs, as illustrated by the lower-right box. In the latter case, citizens receive the policies and institutions demanded, but they fail to maximize social welfare.

For the sake of simplicity, the off-diagonals in Figure 2.3 are assigned a payoff of zero. If policies and institutions are healthy, but the populace does not accept or support them, they will fail to be effective, as illustrated by the off-diagonals. If, for instance, the populace fails to respect—that is, coordinate on—laws regarding private property, then these laws will fail to bind individuals and will be ineffective.

It is also possible that an off-diagonal could yield a positive payoff as well, albeit not as great as if individuals coordinated on good conjectures. For instance, if a government fails to effectively enforce property rights, the populace *may* still informally coordinate on private property norms, but their effectiveness may be severely limited. This is precisely the situation described by Hernando de Soto (1989) in Peru, where informal property rights emerged in the absence of effective formal institutions. However, because the formal institutions fail to align with the emergent informal institutions, the benefits of property rights are constrained in their ability to facilitate the transformation from personal to impersonal exchange.

In reality, only rarely will games of conflict turn into games of pure coordination as illustrated in Figure 2.3. As mentioned earlier, many social interactions lie somewhere between the extreme situations of pure conflict and pure cooperation. For example, if a politician decides to pursue a program of privatization, this will be viewed cooperatively by some of his allies but will be met with resentment by those vested interests that benefit from the status quo. Such situations contain elements of both conflict and cooperation and their location along the overall conflict–coordination spectrum will determine the ability of the parties involved to reach some kind of cooperative agreement.

Like any model, our framework simplifies the process required for policy and institutional changes conducive to economic development. Nonetheless, it captures the process of institutional reform and change, as well as the underlying dilemma facing political agents and citizens in developing countries. Within our framework, successful reforms involve the transformation of potential situations of conflict into situations of coordination. Further, ultimate success requires a solution to the "coordination problem" so that the players involved coordinate around good conjectures which are conducive to economic development.

What is required to transform the situation of conflict depicted in the Reformers' Dilemma in Figure 2.2 to a situation of coordination closer to the game depicted in Figure 2.3 is the identification of mechanisms that approximate the conditions dictated by the folk theorem. In other words, sustainable development requires coordination-enhancing mechanisms that provide the incentive for policymakers to adopt policies and institutions predicated on good conjectures instead of catering to special interest groups. Our contention is that the media is one such mechanism.

MEDIA AS A COORDINATION-ENHANCING MECHANISM

The central argument of this book is that media is a critical element of the broader process of economic development. Further, a free media is the first-best scenario since a free media aids citizens in checking government while simultaneously allowing media to serve as an unhampered mechanism of institutional change and reinforcement. The model developed here illuminates the crucial role that media plays in this process. As we discussed above, the folk theorem indicates that cooperation may be one solution to a multi-period Prisoners' Dilemma if certain conditions hold.

Of course the folk theorem cannot be taken as descriptive of reality given the very specific conditions it requires for cooperation. Nonetheless, it captures the fundamental point that situations of conflict can have cooperative elements if individuals hold the appropriate conjectures.

Given this, the key is finding institutional approximations of the conditions necessary for cooperation according to the folk theorem. A free media is one such institution because it lowers the cost of information sharing and can create shared knowledge among citizens and political agents regarding punishment for defection. To understand the underlying logic, consider why special interest groups are able to narrowly concentrate benefits on their members while dispersing costs on the broader populace. The reason for this is that many citizens tend to remain uninformed about political agents' behavior because obtaining this information is costly relative to citizens' ability to influence political outcomes. As media develops, more information is provided at a lower cost, which shrinks the gap between the marginal benefit and marginal cost of obtaining information regarding special interest group activities. The media serves to aggregate and summarize information, making it readily available to consumers. As the previously mentioned work of Amartya Sen (1984, 1999) emphasizes, the information provided by a free media, especially when coupled with free political competition, provides citizens with the information they need to check political actors' behavior. This indicates that as the media becomes less free, the beneficial information role played by the legal media is reduced.

The media provides a mechanism that can communicate information about political agents' activities—for example whether certain policymakers are engaging in growth-enhancing reform or whether they are engaged in corruption and catering to special interest groups—to large segments of the population. This information may come from political agents interested in "telling on" one another or from the work of journalists who follow politicians' activities. Both sets of actors have an incentive to supply the public with such information provided citizens demand it. The key is that media creates a channel through which this information can be conveyed. Armed with media-provided information about political agents' behavior, citizens are able to more effectively hold defecting policymakers accountable at the voting booth or through other kinds of political resistance and to reward cooperative ones through re-election or through alternative forms of support. By imposing a cost on activities that cater to special interest groups, the threat of citizen punishment enabled by media-provided information creates an incentive for politicians to cooperate on genuine economic reform. In this way, media can help to align the three sets of interests in Figure 2.2, those of competing political actors and the population, by raising each individual policymaker's payoff for committing to pro-development reform above his payoff for catering to special interests.

In addition to providing information about political agents' activities, media also serves to generate common knowledge. For our purposes, the media can facilitate the emergence of two types of common knowledge. The first type emerges around the behavior of politicians within a given set of institutions. As discussed, this allows citizens to punish or reward politicians for the policies they adopt. The second type of common knowledge revolves around the process of institutional change as discussed in the first chapter. Recall that the process of institutional change involves fundamental shifts in the belief systems of members of a society. This process involves those members coordinating on a new belief system equilibrium. As noted, institutional changes can be either gradual or dramatic. In either case, for such institutional changes to be self-sustaining, a large number of individuals must be willing to coordinate on the change. For example, in order for property rights to emerge, people must have some shared understanding of what those rights entail.

No matter which type of common knowledge is at work, widespread coordination is necessary for change to occur. If citizens are going to punish politicians, the undesirable behavior of politicians must be widely known so that a large number of citizens can act accordingly. Likewise, in order to adopt gradual or dramatic institutional change, citizens must be certain that others are going to do the same. The widespread coordination necessary for the disciplining of politicians and for institutional change presents a coordination problem that must be solved.

The easiest way for people to overcome coordination problems is to communicate with one another. But simply communicating is not enough. Since widespread adoption of the norm or rule requires reciprocation, each person must be confident that others will respond in kind. Continuing with the property rights example, each person involved must be confident that if he respects the property of others, his action will be met with in-kind reciprocation. Common knowledge entails each person knowing the relevant information, but also the knowledge that other people know the same information and those other people knowing that others are aware of the information and so forth. When common knowledge exists, people can be confident that everyone involved shares some core information and expectations.

The nineteenth-century French author Alexis de Tocqueville recognized the role of media in producing such common knowledge when he wrote, "Only a newspaper can put the same thought at the same time before a thousand readers . . . A newspaper is not only able to suggest a common plan to many men; it provides them with the means of carrying out in common the plans that they have thought of for themselves" (1835–1840: 517–518). More recently, James Webster and Patricia Phalen note that "it is likely that people watching a media event know that a vast audience is in attendance. Such awareness is part of the event's appeal, and the media are generally eager to report the estimated worldwide attendance" (1997: 120). These authors point out that the media not only informs media consumers directly, but also influences their knowledge and opinions of the information possessed by others. In other words, the media produces common knowledge.

Political scientists have analyzed the importance of finding a solution to the coordination problem for the sustainability of political institutions. For example, Barry Weingast (1995, 1997) emphasizes that the process of citizens establishing limitations on government involves a coordination problem. Simply put, an array of citizens with potentially different views must agree on the appropriate limits of government activity. Weingast contends that an appropriate set of public rules, usually codified in the form of a constitution, can serve as such a coordination device to overcome this problem. He concludes that "a central step in the creation of limited government is that citizens or their representatives construct a mechanism that solves the coordination problem" (1995: 15). Along similar lines, Russell Hardin notes the importance of the coordination problem in establishing and maintaining institutions. He notes that if an "institution is to work relatively well, it must be designed for the citizen with modal incentives to coordinate. And it will likely require backup institutions to enforce its coordination" (1999: 14). The media is one such supporting institution that, "in serving as a coordination device," as Weingast puts it, can reinforce existing institutions while simultaneously contributing to the evolution of those and new institutions.

Our model also illustrates the three effects of media on policy and institutions discussed in Chapter 1. Recall that media can have a gradual effect on policies and institutions by slowly introducing consumers to new ideas, perceptions, and information. In this regard, the media can coordinate citizens and policymakers around new policies and institutions according to the Reformers' Dilemma framework. This process does not lead to wholesale changes in institutions, but rather to marginal changes within an existing institutional framework.

The media can also contribute to an entirely new punctuated equilibrium. The result is significant changes in the very characteristics and constitution of institutions. This is also captured in our model. When a tipping point is reached, existing institutions are unstable and future institutional arrangements are "up for grabs." For example, Olson (1982) notes how a crisis (war, economic crisis, and so on) can generate significant change in political institutions including the collapse of entrenched special-interest coalitions. In such a situation, citizens and political actors will need to coordinate on an entirely new set of institutions. Once a new punctuated equilibrium is achieved, stability returns and the reinforcement and gradual effects once again come into their own.

Finally, the media can also reinforce existing policies and institutions. This is illustrated in the coordination game in Figure 2.3. Once a new policy or institutional equilibrium is achieved, there is no guarantee that it will remain stable over time. However, the media can have a "reinforcement effect" by making a specific equilibrium focal. In this role, the media reinforces an existing equilibrium, making it self-sustaining and self-extending over time.

Note that the Reformers' Dilemma framework captures only a single set of games at a single point in time. In reality, there will often be numerous overlapping games operating at the same time. For example, certain information provided by the media may lead to a divergence between private preferences for change and the status quo. Depending on the magnitude of this divergence, the result may be gradual or punctuated changes in policies and institutions. At the same time, information by the media may reinforce other aspects of existing policies and institutions.

In the next chapter we consider the various factors that influence the effectiveness of media as a coordination-enhancing device. As we will discuss, the state can manipulate the media both directly and indirectly, which may constrain media's ability to overcome the Reformers' Dilemma and coordinate citizens on good conjectures. However, it is important to keep in mind that while a free media is the first-best scenario, even a relatively unfree media can still provide important information to citizens. For example, in some countries where the media is unfree, a large underground media provides citizens with alternative information regarding the behavior of government officials as well as alternative institutional possibilities. In addition to government manipulation of the media, the next chapter also considers how factors such as consumer demand for certain types of information and the quality of information provided may influence the media's effectiveness as a means of coordinating citizens.

THE STYLIZED FACTS OF REFORM AND ECONOMIC DEVELOPMENT

Our Reformers' Dilemma model is consistent with several stylized facts about economic development and changes in policies and institutions.

1. Economic and Institutional Reforms are Possible to Achieve

While institutions are typically stable and durable, one observes cases of dramatic institutional change. The collapse of communism, unanticipated by many, is an example of this. Following this collapse, the record of transition has been mixed. Some countries, such as Estonia, Hungary, and the Czech Republic, have developed relatively quickly compared to other countries in similar situations. In these countries, solutions have been found to the Reformers' Dilemma and politicians and citizens have coordinated on policies and institutions that facilitate economic progress. Once in place, these policies and institutions have been self-enforcing and self-extending.

2. Many Countries Remain in a Continued State of Economic Stagnation and Underdevelopment

There are many countries that have been unable to adopt the institutions found in the developed parts of the world. "Weak states" are one example of this. Countries such as Russia, that have performed relatively poorly following the collapse of communism, are other examples. In these countries, a solution to the Reformers' Dilemma is absent and, as a result, social welfare suffers.

3. A Free Media is a Necessary, but not Sufficient, Condition for Economic Development and Institutional Change

The existing literature shows a correlation between a free media and positive economic outcomes (Djankov *et al.* 2003). All the members of the G-7 (Canada, France, Germany, Italy, Japan, the United Kingdom and the United States), which account for approximately two-thirds of the world's economic output, have a free media (Freedom House 2007). Furthermore, most countries that are considered transition and development "successes"—Estonia, Hungary, and the Czech Republic—have a free media. However, there are many countries that have a free media but remain relatively poor—Benin, Costa Rica, Ghana, Solomon Islands, and so on (Freedom House 2007). Despite a free media, these latter countries have been unable to establish sustainable institutions and adopt good policies that contribute to economic progress.

While a free media is first best and plays an important part in the development process, it is by no means the only part of that process. Other factors, in addition to a free media, also play a role in creating economic progress. These factors include historical experiences, political stability, a stable economic environment outside of the media industry, quality of the media, education, ideology, interest in politics, and willingness to punish ineffective politicians. Stated differently, a free media exists within an existing institutional context. These existing institutions may contribute to the effectiveness of a free media but they may also constrain its effectiveness. Further, once established, an independent media may serve to strengthen some existing institutions but it may also weaken others. It is also important to note that institutional change is an ongoing process and significant change toward sustainable institutions conducive to economic development can take years if not generations. A free media is by no means a guarantee of immediate economic development.

4. The Adoption of Policies and Institutions Conducive to Economic Development Requires the Creation of Common Knowledge Around a Certain Set of Conjectures

Media serves a dual role in development. First, it provides citizens with information regarding the policies adopted by policymakers. From this standpoint, media serves as a check on politicians. Second, media can introduce citizens to new information, ideas, and perceptions which influence their belief systems. In this role, the media can serve as a catalyst of gradual and dramatic change. In both cases, the media can generate common knowledge allowing for a solution to the broader coordination problem.

Note that the transformation of the Reformers' Dilemma in Figure 2.2 into the coordination game in Figure 2.3 is not by itself sufficient for economic development. Coordination can take place around both good and bad conjectures. These possibilities will generate very different outcomes. Economic progress requires the transformation of situations of conflict to cooperation around good conjectures that support economic development. While there are many different ways to live, there are very few ways to live prosperously. As mentioned at the outset of this chapter, the policies and institutions necessary for economic development and progress are well known. The challenge for underdeveloped countries is finding a solution to the Reformers' Dilemma that allows for the adoption of such policies and institutions.

5. Media Can Serve as a Catalyst of Change *and* as a Mechanism of Reinforcement

Institutions are characterized by their stability and durability. However, one does observe cases where institutional change is dramatic and widespread. In these instances, the very constitution of institutions and institutional arrangements changes. The Reformers' Dilemma framework, as well as our focus on media as a mechanism of change and reinforcement, helps solve this apparent paradox.

The Reformers' Dilemma captures that fact that political actors often lack an incentive to adopt beneficial policies and institutions. It also illustrates that certain mechanisms can provide the necessary incentive for reformers to act in the best interests of their citizens, leading to changes in policies and institutions. Finally, it captures the coordination problem inherent in policy and institutional changes. In short, reformers must have an incentive to adopt reforms and there must be mechanisms to coordinate people around those reforms both prior to adoption and after they are in place.

The media can create common knowledge around existing institutions and policies that can have a reinforcement effect on existing arrangements. At the same time, the media can introduce consumers to new ideas and perceptions that can lead to gradual change. Once these gradual changes reach a potential tipping point due to an increasing preference gap between private and public preferences, dramatic change is possible. Sustainable development requires the adoption of certain policies and institutions—the gradual and punctuation effects of media—*and* the reinforcement of those policies and institutions once in place—the reinforcement effect of media. The central issue becomes understanding the factors that influence the strength of the three effects of media on policies and institutions.

ACKNOWLEDGEMENTS

This chapter draws on Coyne and Leeson (2004) and Leeson and Coyne (2007). Coyne (2007) develops a similar model to analyze the process of postwar reconstruction and the transformation of situations of conflict to cooperation.

NOTES

1. No assumptions are made regarding the gender of any of the actors in the book. 'He' and 'She' are used at random to avoid cumbersome phraseology.
2. Though we do not model them explicitly, this game also reflects the interest of special interest groups, which are benefited equally when either or both political agents cater to them, and are harmed when both political agents own policy.
3. This framework is based on Leeson (2006), who developed it to explain why even partially-benevolent politicians under democracy fail to deliver social welfare enhancing policy.

REFERENCES

Coyne, Christopher J. (2007) *After War: The Political Economy of Exporting Democracy*. Palo Alto, CA: Stanford University Press.

Coyne, Christopher J. and Peter T. Leeson (2004) "Read All About It! Understanding the Role of Media in Economic Development," *Kyklos*, 57: 21–44.

De Soto, Hernando (1989) *The Other Path*. New York: Basic Books.

Djankov, Simeon, Caralee McLiesh, Tatiana Nenova, and Andrei Shleifer (2003) "Who Owns the Media?" *Journal of Law and Economics*, 46: 341–382.

Freedom House (2007) *Freedom of the Press 2007: A Global Survey of Media Independence*. New York: Rowman and Littlefield.

Gwartney, James, Randall Holcombe, and Robert Lawson (1999) "Economic Freedom and the Environment for Economic Growth," *Journal of Institutional and Theoretical Economics*, 155: 1–21.

Hanke, Steve and Stephen Walters (1997) "Economic Freedom, Prosperity and Equality," *Cato Journal*, 17: 117–146.

Hardin, Russell (1999) *Liberalism, Constitutionalism, and Democracy*. New York: Oxford University Press.

Leeson, Peter T. (2006) "How Much Benevolence is Benevolent Enough?" *Public Choice*, 126: 357–366.

Leeson, Peter T. and Christopher J. Coyne (2007) "The Reformers' Dilemma: Media, Policy Ownership, and Reform," *European Journal of Law and Economics*, 23: 237–250.

Olson, Mancur (1982) *The Rise and Decline of Nations*. New Haven, CT: Yale University Press.

Rodrik, Dani (2007) *One Economics Many Recipes: Globalization, Institutions, and Economic Growth*. Princeton, NJ: Princeton University Press.

Scully, Gerald (1988) "The Institutional Framework and Economic Development," *Journal of Political Economy*, 96: 652–662.

Schelling, Thomas (1960) *The Strategy of Conflict*. New York: Oxford University Press.

Sen, Amartya (1984) *Poverty and Famines*. Oxford: Oxford University Press.

Sen, Amartya (1999) *Development as Freedom*. New York: Alfred A. Knopf Inc.

Smith, Adam (1775) [1937] "Notes on the Wealth of Nations," as reported in the editors' Introduction to *An Inquiry into the Nature and Causes of the Wealth of Nations*, New York: Modern Library.

Tocqueville, Alexis de (1835–1840 [1988]) *Democracy in America*. New York: Harper Perennial.

Tullock, Gordon (1999) "Non-Prisoner's Dilemma," *Journal of Economic Behavior and Organization*, 39: 455–458.

Webster, James G. and Patricia F. Phalen (1997). *The Mass Audience: Rediscovering the Dominant Model*. Mahwah, NJ: Lawrence Erlbaum Associates.

Weingast, Barry R. (1995) "The Economic Role of Political Institutions: Market-Preserving Federalism and Economic Development," *Journal of Law, Economics and Organization* 11(1): 1–31.

Weingast, Barry R. (1997) "The Political Foundations of Democracy and the Rule of Law," *American Political Science Review*, 91(2): 245–263.

3. The determinants of media effectiveness

INTRODUCTION

Media serves a critical role in a free society by checking government and generating the common knowledge necessary for the change and reinforcement of policies and institutions. However, the effectiveness of media in these roles varies across societies and countries. What factors contribute to the effectiveness of media? Our goal in this chapter is to explore the answer to this question. We analyze four main determinants that influence the effectiveness of the media. In each case we make the connection between the factor under consideration and the Reformers' Dilemma model developed in Chapter 2, as well as the impact of these factors on the three effects of media—gradual, punctuation and reinforcement—discussed in Chapter 1. Specifically, we consider how each determinant influences media as a check on government actors and as a mechanism of policy and institutional change.

The first factor we consider is government intervention in the media industry. We identify four main avenues through which government can manipulate the media and consider the impact of those manipulations on the media's effectiveness as a credible check on government. We also consider how government manipulation influences the divergence between private and public preferences for change. We then turn our focus to the legal environment in which media outlets must operate. Our main focus here is on laws regarding the availability of information, as well as laws protecting journalists and media employees from threats, intimidation and lawsuits. The third factor we analyze is the quality of the media. Even a free media must have competent journalists and employees to effectively report and manage the day-to-day operations of media outlets. We consider issues such as journalist ethics, integrity, and bias. Finally, we examine the economic factors influencing the media industry. A media outlet is a business just like any other and, as such, is subject to the general economic conditions of the country it operates in. Thus we consider the array of economic factors influencing the profitability of media outlets.

Although we present these four determinants of media effectiveness as distinct and separate categories, in practice they are not always independent from one another. There is interplay and overlap between the factors considered. For instance, government manipulation of the media through taxation or fees will also impact the economic conditions that media outlets face. Likewise, the legal environment, which includes information and transparency laws, as well as laws protecting journalists, may be the subject of government manipulation. In discussing each factor we are careful to highlight and emphasize the overlap with the other determinants of media effectiveness.

GOVERNMENT MANIPULATION OF THE MEDIA

The existing literature in the area of media and economic development analyzes the impact of various ownership structures (private versus state) on economic outcomes, as well as the importance of media as a check on government (Besley and Burgess 2002; Djankov *et al.* 2003). The latter note that a number of factors may be important in determining the extent of media manipulation, but except for outlet ownership, do not explore them. Besley and Prat (2006), on the other hand, explore the impact of media capture by government but do not investigate the specific ways that this media capture can occur. Missing, then, is an analysis of *how* government manipulates the media. In other words, what methods does the state use to influence the content of media-provided information? Is dependence limited strictly to media outlets, or does it extend to media-related infrastructure as well? Are privately owned media outlets free from state influence? If not, how does government influence these media?

We argue that there are four specific channels through which government manipulates the media environment: 1) *direct* control via outlet ownership, 2) *indirect* control via infrastructure ownership, 3) *indirect* control via financial pressure, and 4) *indirect* control via entry regulation. We will consider each channel in turn and then discuss government manipulation in the context of the Reformers' Dilemma model.

Direct Control via State-Owned Media Outlets

As Grossman and Hart (1986) point out, ownership bestows control. Thus, in the case of explicitly state-owned media outlets, it is not difficult to imagine how government influences media-provided information. These outlets are financed entirely by the state and consequently do not rely upon consumers to remain afloat. Since they are beholden to the state for funding, state-owned media outlets have a strong incentive to avoid being critical of the current government. Furthermore, as state-owned enterprises, these outlets are run exclusively by government-appointed directors, who determine both the stories that will be covered, and the light in which these stories will be conveyed. Politicians in power thus choose directors and editors that will do their bidding, creating heavily biased news. Government's manipulation of media-provided information is obvious in this case.

There are numerous examples of state ownership from around the world. For instance, in Myanmar the largest television station is controlled by the Ministry of Information and the second largest station is directly controlled by the Myanmar military. In Turkmenistan, the state owns and controls the entire press. In Kenya, the government controls the Kenyan Broadcasting Corporation (KBC). In North Korea, all aspects of the media are controlled by the Korean Workers' Party and the affiliated government agencies. These are but a few examples of state-owned media.

Closely related to direct state ownership of media outlets is the ownership of outlets by incumbent politicians. A phenomenon called "Berlusconization," whereby political leaders purchase media outlets to use for their political purposes, is a common method of this form of government media manipulation. This practice received its name from Italian Prime Minister Silvio Berlusconi, who is also a prominent Italian media mogul, and refers to the endowment of media ownership and a political office in the same individual. Although in this case outlets are technically in the hands of private owners, they are acquired and operated for the purposes of manipulating information reaching the outlet's audience. In many instances these outlets are not even self-sustaining but are instead cross-subsidized by their owners' other businesses that generate profits.

Examples of this type of hybrid private–public ownership are common. In Saudi Arabia, for example, several members of the royal family own controlling shares in two of the five most popular daily papers. Likewise, in Kazakhstan, the daughter and son-in-law of President Nazarbayev own seven major media outlets. The prime minister of Ukraine owns 30 per cent of the country's main television station. In Kenya the Kenyan African National Union, which ruled the country from 1963 to 2002, owned the fourth largest daily paper, the *Kenya Times* (Djankov *et al.* 2003: 351, 353).

It is also important to note that in many countries there is a mix of state and private ownership. One example of this is the British Broadcasting Corporation (BBC). This is the largest broadcasting corporation in the world as measured by audience size. Officially the BBC is characterized as a state-owned but independent corporation. The BBC Trust oversees its operation and is, at least in theory, independent of political influence. However, it is important to note that the appointment process of the trustees is political in nature. Trustees are officially appointed by the Queen based on the advice of ministers. The entire process is regulated by the Office of the Commissioner for Public Appointments. The BBC coexists with numerous private media outlets, and in general the United Kingdom is considered to have a free media. This serves to illustrate the common mix in many countries between both state and private ownership. The media landscape of a country is often not characterized as completely state-owned or completely private, but rather by some mix of the two. The central question then becomes the magnitude, extent, and nature of state ownership versus private ownership.

Indirect Control via State-Owned Media Infrastructure

The American journalist A.J. Liebling once said: "Freedom of the press is guaranteed only to those who own one" (1960: 9). Liebling's remark is insightful because it highlights the importance of the ownership of the inputs used in media production. If media outlets are privately owned but vital means of production and distribution are monopolized in the hands of the state, government's control over the media remains strong.

The case of Romania illustrates how state ownership of media-related infrastructure is one indirect method government can use to manipulate the media. For many years following the end of communism in Romania, there was only one newsprint mill in the country—Letea SA Bacau—a state-owned firm. The government's monopoly on newsprint gave it direct control over what private newspapers would be able to operate, and through this indirect control over the content of paper-reported news.

Similarly, until 2003, the major distribution network for printed media in Romania was Rodipet, a state-owned firm. Rodipet functioned as one of government's strongest structural controls over the printed media industry in Romania. The state was able to use its monopoly position over distribution in much the same way that it was able to use its former monopoly position over newsprint to indirectly control what information reached the public. For instance, after a newspaper owner in the county of Braila with strong connections to the mayor was appointed general manager of Rodipet in his region, Rodipet stopped distributing two competing independent papers in the city (IREX 2002: 82).

Yet another means of indirect government control through infrastructure is state ownership of news agencies. These are organizations of journalists and reporters that supply information to the news trade—newspapers, magazines, radio, television, and so on. They prepare news stories that can then be used by media outlets with little or no modifica-tion. As such, news agencies are a key part of the media industry infra-structure. State ownership of news agencies will influence the details and reporting of stories and news provided to the news trade, which will then be passed on to consumers. The Associated Press of Pakistan, for example, is government-owned and operated.

A final means of indirect government control of the media through government involvement with media infrastructure is the allowing of private media ownership but only in partnership with the government. This dynamic is evident in Vietnam, where the media industry is viewed as a joint undertaking between private individuals and the state. For example, private individuals may own newspapers but state agencies are typically responsible for the publication of the paper. An example of this is the *Vietnam Investment Review.* This paper is foreign-owned by a private entrepreneur but published by the State Committee for Cooperation and Investment. Along similar lines, the main dailies in Vietnam are all either state-owned or affiliated with a government agency that controls the infra-structure needed to produce the paper (Panol and Do 2000: 474).

Indirect Control via Financial Pressure

There is great truth in the old adage of not biting the hand that feeds you. Where media is independent of government, this means avoiding the ire of its customers. Where media outlets rely upon government to remain afloat, however, it means staying on the good side of those who wield political power. By creating an environment in which most private media outlets depend financially upon the state, government is able to indirectly control the media.

As we will discuss in the subsequent section on the economic factors influencing media, in many developing countries, the government is an easy source of funding for struggling media outlets. However, this reliance on the political apparatus for financial support allows members of the gov-ernment to manipulate and influence the media. Along these lines, Dragan Janic, the editor-in-chief of Beta News Agency, noted that the economic problems facing media outlets in Serbia meant that these outlets "become an easy prey of politicians" who offer them financial support (quoted in Carrington and Nelson 2002: 226).

The government can also manipulate the media through tax policy. For example, consider the tax policies in use by the Romanian government in 2001. Among other taxes, Romanian businesses were required to pay a 19 per cent value-added tax, a 25 per cent tax on corporate profits, and a 52 per cent tax on their gross payroll. In addition to this, media outlets

Table 3.1   Private TV station debt to the Romanian government—2004

Private TV Station	Debt to State (USD)
Ameron Television SRL	8 506 898
Antena 1 SA	1 925 886
Corporatia Pentru Cultura SI Arta Intact SA	1 708 567
Media Pro International SA*	7 809 797
Rieni Drinks SA	1 540 018
Scandic Distilleries SA	1 438 380
Rosul Group SRL	548 216

Note: It is worth noting that Media Pro owns Mediafax, the largest news agency in Romania

Source: Ministry of Public Finance, 2004, as reported by the Romanian Academic Society (2004)

in particular were burdened by a 3–11 per cent advertising tax, which in conjunction with these others made the profitability of operating in the media business extremely low (IREX 2001: 179).[1] Romania's generally excessive tax environment created a situation in which many media outlets could not afford to stay in business without going into debt to government. For example, in 2003, ProTV, Romania's largest private television station, owed close to $50 million in unpaid taxes (Freedom House 2003: 128). In fact, only a few years ago, *every* national private television station in Romania was significantly indebted to the government (Romanian Academic Society 2004). Table 3.1 illustrates some of this debt as recently acknowledged by the Romanian Ministry of Finance.

The government can use this debt to pressure media outlets *not* to cover particular stories, to address issues from an angle that will favor those in power, or to give disproportionate airtime to the governing party. The Media Monitoring Agency, for example, monitored the top four Romanian television stations for one week in May 2002 and found that 78 per cent of all political coverage was of ruling party leaders while only 22 per cent covered opposition leaders (2002: 26). In a similar study that looked at the period between 27 June 2003 and 6 July 2003, the then Romanian Prime Minister Adrian Nastase and President Iliescu comprised together a full 80 per cent of all political appearances on prime time television news bulletins (Media Monitoring Agency 2004: 5).

Advertising is yet another way that government can indirectly manipulate the media. It is a key component of the revenues of media outlets in all countries. In many developing countries private media outlets must rely heavily upon state-purchased advertisements to remain in business.

Government can use this financial power to pressure media sources to bias reported information such that it favors the governing party. The result of this indirect pressure is a reduction in the accuracy and credibility of media outlets.

Regulation forms another important method of financial pressure that government uses to manipulate the media. In many developing countries, political leaders take advantage of excessive and ambiguous regulations that restrict the general business environment in their country. These regulations empower politicians to find real or imaginary financial and operational violations by media outlets that refuse to do their bidding. Alleged violations are then used to financially or operationally strangle unfriendly media sources via hefty fines, raising the cost of compliance so high as to prevent profitability, or achieve outright closure of outlets. Government can also use the threat of infraction to blackmail media sources into biasing news coverage. The dynamics of the abuse of ambiguous regulations will vary from case to case and may involve punishing uncooperative media outlets via audits, punitive taxation, or through pressuring their main subscribers, among other abuses.

Indirect Control via Entry Regulation

As Djankov *et al.* (2003) point out, politicians benefit by regulating firms' entry into particular industries. In the case of the media industry this is particularly true. By acting as the gatekeeper to the media industry, government can keep out potential media providers who might be hostile toward its policies and throw out existing media producers who do not serve its ends. In this way entry regulation gives government a powerful method of indirectly manipulating mass media. The main form of entry regulation takes place through the process of licensing. This can impact both media outlets as a whole and the journalists who work for those media outlets. Government officials can control the media industry either by preventing media outlets and journalists from initially obtaining a license to enter the industry, or by failing to renew existing licenses.

To understand how licensing restricts the number of media outlets, consider the case of South Korea in the 1960s. In the 1940s and 1950s, the government regulated the newspaper industry through a licensing process to prevent the publication of progressive and critical papers. When the licensing process was eased in the 1960s, the number of daily newspapers increased dramatically along with the variety in coverage in terms of topics, opinions and viewpoints. Specifically, the number of daily newspapers increased from 41 to 112 while the number of news agencies increased from 14 to 274 (Heo, Uhm and Chang 2000: 614).

Along similar lines, consider the case of Taiwan. With the rise of the communist party in the late 1940s, a freeze on newspaper licenses was implemented along with a ceiling on the length of newspapers. For the next three and a half decades, the number of newspapers remained constant at 31 while each issue was limited to 12 pages. The government used the license freeze to ban ownership of media outlets by opposition parties. Those outlets that did have a license were careful not to criticize the incumbents for fear of losing their license. The freeze on newspaper licenses and the ceiling on issue length were lifted in 1988. The market quickly responded. The number of newspapers increased from 31 in 1987 to 360 in 1998. Further, the number of pages in the most popular newspapers increased from 12 up to 50 (Wang and Lo 2000: 663).

Most recently, consider the case of Radio Caracas Television (RCTV) in Venezuela. As part of his broader effort to nationalize key industries, President Hugo Chavez refused to renew the license of RCTV in May 2006. RCTV had been on the air for 53 years and was the most watched television station in the country. More importantly, it was the main platform for political opposition to Chavez to air their views and opinions. Chavez claimed that RCTV violated broadcasting laws and supported the 2002 coup against him. Critics contend that the real reason behind the failure of Chavez to renew the license was to silence the voice of any opposition to his regime. RCTV will be replaced by a state-owned station that is controlled by the Chavez administration. The closure of RCTV leaves only one smaller private cable station, Globalvisión, which has hosted opposition views in the past. However, two days after closing RCTV, Chavez threatened Globalvisión, saying, "I recommend they ponder very carefully how far they want to go" (quoted in *Economist* 2007b: 39). Given the precedent set by the closing of RCTV, one should not expect to see much opposition reporting from Globalvisión for fear of not having its license renewed.

Another form of entry regulation is the licensing of journalists. Where such licensing procedures exist, it is illegal for unlicensed individuals to practice journalism. There is an ongoing debate regarding the benefits and costs associated with journalist licensing. The argument has been made that licensing creates a set of standards that fosters journalist responsibility and ethics. Against this position there is the real possibility, especially in developing countries with weak or absent checks on government, that licensing will be used as a punishment device by government agents. More specifically, the threat is that the government will utilize the licensing process to censor those journalists that may be, or have been, critical of the government. This censorship may take place during the initial licensing process or during the renewal process. In either case, if the licensing process is used to censor dissenting or critical views, it curtails the effectiveness of media.

Media Manipulation and the Reformers' Dilemma

Napoleon once said: "If I were to give liberty to the press, my power could not last three days" (quoted in Frank 2003: 157). Clearly he understood the power of media in checking the abuses of political rulers. Furthermore, Napoleon's remark suggests that a free media would have made a difference for France's economy and overall development. If he were correct, an independent media would have served as a check and forced him to change his policies or be thrown from power. This policy difference would in turn have generated a markedly different French economy.

As this line of reasoning indicates, media manipulation primarily affects economic performance and development indirectly through its impact on which policies and institutions are adopted. What policies and institutions are adopted is in turn a function of the behavior of those in political power.

As we discussed in Chapter 2, policies and institutions broadly tend to serve one of two interests: public or private. Policies and institutions that serve public interests are those that generally raise the long-run living standard of a country's entire range of inhabitants, or at least do not disproportionately benefit one small group at the expense of everyone else. Such policies and institutions are those typically considered growth enhancing and necessary for economic prosperity. They include, for instance, property protection, low inflation, low taxes, transparent regulation, stable rule of law, and free trade. Policies and institutions that serve private interests, in contrast, are those generally aimed at privileging a small class of individuals at the expense of the rest of society. In the absence of a mechanism that punishes them for doing so, politicians prefer to create this kind of policy because it serves their own interests.

Independent media-provided information increases the transparency of the policy-making process, and accurately reveals to voters which politicians support public-oriented policies and institutions, and which support private-oriented ones. By correctly informing citizens about politicians' activities, an independent media makes these activities common knowledge and enables voters to effectively monitor politicians at low cost (Besley and Burgess 2002; Besley and Prat 2006). This creates an incentive for politicians to adopt policies and institutions that serve public rather than private interests, as they are aware that if they do not, voters will find out and punish them accordingly at election time. In the context of the Reformers' Dilemma model, an independent media is a mechanism that can raise the benefits of cooperation around "good conjectures" compared to defecting by serving private interests. Stated differently, an independent media raises the cost of defection by monitoring politicians' behaviors.

An independent media is also critical because it tends to provide credible information that can be trusted by consumers. In other words, consumers can be confident that they are not receiving information that has been biased by the government in one direction or the other. Where the media is manipulated by the state this mechanism breaks down. The breakdown occurs by affecting the dissemination of credible information.

State-manipulated media tends to take two specific forms: 1) information withholding, in which the state prevents media outlets from disseminating unfavorable news, and 2) misinformation, in which the state uses its control to bias news in a way that favors incumbent politicos, or to fabricate untruthful news that will favor these actors. If citizens do not receive relevant information about the policy behavior of politicians, or receive false information about this behavior, then the monitoring capacity of media is compromised and the information it provides cannot be used as the basis for punishment. This means two negative things for policy and institutions. On the one hand, politicians who refuse to pursue policies and institutions in the public's interest will not be effectively weeded out by citizens. Furthermore, if political agents know this, they have an additional incentive to indulge in the creation of policies and institutions that serve private rather than public ends. Under such circumstances the media will fail to serve as an effective solution to the Reformers' Dilemma and as a tool for policy and institutional change around good conjectures fostering economic development.

The harmful effects of media manipulation can be divided into "objective" consequences on the one hand, and "subjective" consequences on the other. The objective consequences of media manipulation are those described above. As a result of state manipulation, less information and/or less accurate information about the behavior of politicians and political happenings reaches the public, compromising citizens' ability to use the media to hold unscrupulous political agents accountable. We call these consequences of media manipulation "objective" because their occurrence is independent of citizens' knowledge about the status of information manipulation in their country. The subjective consequences of media manipulation, in contrast, are those that depend on citizens' awareness of the extent of media manipulation in their country. The primary subjective consequence we have in mind here is what we call manipulated media's "credibility crisis." Consumers who are aware that the information reaching them is filtered may lose their trust in media-provided information, discounting even accurate information that reaches them because they can never be certain of its credibility.

The subjective consequences of media manipulation thus strengthen its deleterious objective effects described above.

Although the distinction between the objective and subjective consequences of government manipulated media is an important one, it is equally important to appreciate the inextricable connection between the two. Manipulated media's credibility crisis (that is, its subjective consequences) is a direct effect of the objective consequences of state-manipulated media. Without the objective results of media manipulation—less/inaccurate information—there would be no credibility problem for citizens to become aware of (that is, no subjective consequences).

Assuming that citizens are able to participate in the political process, their inability to make informed political decisions as a result of media's dependence upon the state leaves politicians largely unaccountable to the public. Unable to use media to effectively monitor politicians' behavior, citizens remain relatively powerless to punish political agents who serve private rather than public interests. Knowing this, political agents pursue policies and institutions that serve private ends. Thus, instead of simplifying business regulations to reduce their number and opaqueness, or accelerating privatization efforts, for instance, regulations grow and privatization efforts are stalled. Although politicians, bureaucrats, and a small number of existing businesses benefit from this, the Reformers' Dilemma persists and the vast majority of society is harmed. Ultimately, this serves to reinforce "bad" policies and institutions, making change in future periods that much more difficult.

There is an important connection between media manipulation and the three effects of media discussed in Chapter 1. As noted, when the government owns the media, rulers use it to reinforce their power. This has a negative impact on society as bad policies and institutions sustain and become increasingly entrenched over time. However, although unintended on the part of the ruling elite, the reinforcement effect can have the unintended consequence of driving a wedge between private and public preferences. This dynamic operates as follows.

Where the state controls media it will tend to use it to reinforce its position of power and squash opposing views and perceptions. However, if the private preferences of citizens differ from public preferences, a preference gap exists. As the divergence between accurate private preferences and inaccurate public preferences grows, so too does the preference gap. At some point, the wedge between private and public preference results in a potential tipping point. If this tipping point is acted on, it may ultimately lead to punctuated change, removing existing rulers from power. Under such circumstances, by controlling the media to preserve their power, governments can sow the seeds of their own demise.

In sum, where government manipulates the media industry, the reinforcement effect will typically be strong as government actors attempt to reinforce their hold on power. However, this does not preclude the possibility of gradual and punctuated change as government reinforcement can have the unintended consequences of undermining existing policies and institutions through a growing preference gap. The case studies of Poland and Russia in Chapter 5 illustrate this logic.

LEGAL ENVIRONMENT

In this section we focus on the legal structure as it applies to transparency through the availability of information and the protection of journalists from political intimidation and violence. Both are critical factors in the effectiveness of the media. If journalists do not have access to information they cannot report on government activities in a timely manner, if at all. As such, the role of media as a check on government activities will be significantly weakened. Likewise, if journalists can be threatened, intimidated or arrested they will be unable to report relevant news for fear of negative repercussions. Given this, the protection of journalists is a key factor in the effectiveness of the media. In addition to reducing the ability of the media to check political actors, the legal environment will also influence media's ability as a mechanism of policy and institutional change. Where the legal environment prevents access to information or does not protect journalists, the media will be limited in its ability to introduce new ideas and information to consumers. Ultimately, this will distort the process of policy and institutional change that requires changes in the belief systems and mental models of the members of a society.

Information and Transparency

Access to timely and accurate information is important for several reasons. At the most basic level it allows media outlets to report on current events and happenings. Further, accurate and verifiable records allow media outlets to hold government officials accountable while ensuring that the information they report is credible. Absent accurate information, media outlets will suffer from credibility issues because consumers cannot be sure that the information being communicated is accurate. This lack of credibility may also extend to the government itself as the trust of citizens will be lacking where government is not transparent. Finally, openness and the availability of information foster an environment of competition between media sources to obtain and report that information quickly, accurately and effectively. There is an inherent check in such an environment because information is readily verifiable by other media sources. Hence, those who misrepresent the facts will be weeded out more quickly in an environment of openness and transparency.

Given this, an effective media requires the development of minimal laws which allows the development of information markets (Krug and Price 2002: 188). However, the legal structure need not be perfectly defined. Once media has access to some degree of government information it will tend to continue to pressure government agents to increase transparency, strengthening previous laws and seeking to broaden the scope of such laws. The continuous development of these information markets in turn relies on fast and easy access to public information. Developing countries that have made the most progress—specifically those in Central and Eastern Europe—have effectively undertaken media privatization and policies that allow the media industry to take hold through the development of information markets (Carrington and Nelson 2002: 243).

In many countries freedom of information laws, which provide for access to government information and documents, are formally legislated. The limits set by these laws vary from country to country as do the enforcement of the laws. However, as David Banisar notes, "Many of the laws are not adequate and promote access in name only. In some countries, the laws lie dormant due to a failure to implement them properly or a lack of demand. In others, the exemptions and fees are abused by governments" (2006: 6).

From a regional perspective, countries in the Middle East are the worst in terms of the adoption and enforcement of freedom of information laws; only Israel has such a law in place. Freedom of information laws exist in much of Europe, with Russia and Belarus being the only larger countries without them. The laws of other countries in Europe, including Italy, Greece, and Spain, are in place but are considered dysfunctional due to lack of effective enforcement. Many countries in the Americas have similar laws in place or have recently adopted them. For instance, freedom of information laws are now in place in Antigua, Barbuda, the Dominican Republic, Ecuador, Jamaica, Mexico, Trinidad and Tobago, Belize, Panama, and Peru. It remains to be seen if these laws will be executed in a manner that allows media outlets to obtain information in a timely manner. In Africa and the Asia-Pacific regions, the adoption of laws has been slower. Australia, Hong Kong, New Zealand, South Korea, and Thailand have effective laws in place. Most of the countries in Africa, in contrast, are lacking even basic freedom of information laws (Banisar 2006: 19–20).

To understand why the mere existence of information laws is necessary but not sufficient, consider that many existing laws allow government officials to delay the dissemination of information to the media and public. Even where laws regarding transparency are in place, if government officials can delay responding to requests, the effectiveness of the information laws will be hampered. Delays in responding to requests for information can either be intentional or unintentional. In the latter case, delays are due to ineffective administration and bureaucracy. Unintentional delays are a problem in even the most developed countries. For instance, some requests in the United Kingdom and the United States, two countries with well-established freedom of information laws, can take up to a year to process (Banisar 2006: 28). These problems can be worse in developing countries where laws are not as strong and bureaucracies are more inefficient.

Intentional delays refer to efforts by government officials to slow the process of releasing information to the public. The ability to intentionally delay information renders transparency laws useless because information will not be released in a timely manner. Given this, to be effective, information transparency laws must contain a system of checks to ensure that government officials cannot intentionally delay requests for information. Further, there must be an effective process for administering requests, or transparency laws will be ineffective. For example, there must be clear guidelines for media members to submit information requests and a process must be put in place for handling complaints regarding unprocessed or rejected requests.

To understand some of the dynamics discussed above, consider the case of Pakistan. In 1997, the government introduced the Freedom of Information Ordinance, which allowed citizens access to public records while obligating the government to provide details on government activities and decisions. However, the ordinance lapsed within the year and left the country without any effective transparency laws (Ali and Gunaratne 2000: 176–177). In October 2002, Pakistan President Pervez Musharraf supported the Freedom of Information Ordinance 2002. The law has remained on the books but with very weak or non-existent rules and processes for utilizing the law. For instance, it is unclear what information is accessible or what steps are required to obtain information (Banisar 2006: 118–119). As this example illustrates, the effectiveness of freedom of information laws will be curtailed when complementary rules and guidelines allowing members of the media and public to use the law are absent.

In contrast to Pakistan, consider the case of the Philippines. The right to information was included in the 1973 Constitution and expanded in 1987. Further, there is a precedent of transparency in the Philippines dating back to 1948 when the Supreme Court recognized the right of the public to access information related to the government. Although there is no official freedom of information law on the books, the combination of the constitution and precedent created by prior Supreme Court decisions has made the media in the Philippines one of the most open in the region. There is a set of formal and informal guidelines and rules in place for requesting information and appealing requests that are rejected or delayed. While far from perfect, this set of checks and appeals does provide citizens some means of recourse. There are also three independent press monitoring agencies which, though they have no official legal standing, serve as an important check on media outlets and government agencies (Maslog 2000: 379–380; Banisar 2006: 122–124).

As the examples of Pakistan and the Philippines show, there is a large grey area regarding transparency and freedom of information. As Pakistan illustrates, the presence of a formal freedom of information law is no guarantee of transparency. Absent effective complementary rules and guidelines, a formal information law is useless. On the other hand, as the Philippines demonstrates, even in the absence of a formal freedom of information law, historical precedent may serve to foster transparency of information. In general, the problems associated with information transparency will constrain the effectiveness of the media and an adequate solution to these problems must be found to maximize media's potential to serve as a check on government and as a mechanism for creating legitimacy around policy and institutional change.

Journalist and Media Protection

For the media to be effective in overcoming the Reformers' Dilemma, journalists and media employees must be protected from frivolous lawsuits, threats, intimidation, and violence. A lack of protection from coercion will obviously change the behavior of media employees, who will be hesitant to report on certain topics or issues. There are numerous direct and indirect ways media employees can be harassed and intimidated. In this section we consider some of the most prevalent forms of coercion.

Insult laws are a primary means of coercing journalists and media employees in over 100 countries around the world (Walden 2002: 207). Insult laws are statutes that make it illegal to insult government or those holding positions in government. The specific nature of these laws varies from country to country. Some make it illegal to criticize certain government officials (for example, religious leaders, or a royal family) while others make it illegal to criticize or "insult" any government official. Despite the differences across insult laws, what they have in common is that they elevate the government and government officials above criticism.

In doing so, they significantly reduce media's effectiveness as a check on the government and as a mechanism for generating credibility around policy and institutional change. Insult laws stifle critical discussion, dissent, and hence the accountability of government officials. Some specific examples will help clarify the variety of insult laws around the world.

In August 2006, a Rwandan journalist was found guilty of "public insult" for a series of articles that criticized the government's operation. The newspaper editor, Charles Kabonero, was fined one million Rwandan francs (approximately $1800) and was given a one-year suspended prison sentence (Greene 2006: 159). In Zambia, the government is attempting to deport Roy Clarke, a British writer, for referring to President Levy Mwanawasa as "a fool" in an article written over two years ago and published in an independent paper. The Zambian government had already been successful in deporting Smart Edward, a British national, for "defaming" the president. It was argued the Edward was "likely to be a danger to peace and good order" (Greene 2006: 166–167).

In February 2006, José Ovidio Rodríguez Cuesta, known as Napoleón Bravo, of Venevisión TV, was charged with defaming the Venezuelan Superior Court and the entire judicial system during his television program. If he had been found guilty, Rodríguez faced up to 15 months in prison. Also in Venezuela, journalist Julio Balza was sentenced to two years and 11 months in prison for defaming Minister Ramón Alonzo Carrizalez Rengifo. In addition to the prison sentence, Balza must pay approximately $12 500 in reparations. Balza was sued by Carrizalez, the Minister of Infrastructure, for criticizing his performance after a public bridge collapsed (Greene 2006: 207–208).

Similarly, in Kazakhstan, Yermurat Bapi, editor of the Kazakh opposition paper *SolDat*, was convicted of "publicly insulting the dignity and honor" of the President Nursultan Nazarbayev. The charges stemmed from an article reprinted in *SolDat* regarding alleged corruption involving the President and other top-ranking officials in the Kazakh government. The editor was sentenced to a year in prison and fined approximately $280 (Walden 2002: 211). In Algeria, the cartoonist Ali Dilem was given a one-year prison sentence and fined $700 for insulting President Abdelaziz Bouteflika through a series of caricatures that appeared in a local paper. In another case in Algeria, a freelance journalist, Arezki Aït-Larbi, was sentenced, without his knowledge, to six months in prison for defamation of the Justice Ministry for a 1995 article he wrote criticizing the Ministry for its response to charges of detainee treatment. Aït-Larbi learned about the sentence when he went to renew his passport and a background check was initiated (Greene 2006: 259–260).

These are only a few examples of cases involving insult laws. There are many more from countries around the world. This issue of insult laws came to the forefront in September 2005 when the Danish newspaper *Jyllands-Posten* published twelve editorial cartoons depicting the Islamic prophet Muhammad. The cartoons generated global protest and kicked off a fierce debate over the limits of free speech as they relate to "hate speech" and insult. Denmark has vague laws against hate speech on the books, but Denmark's chief public prosecutor announced in March 2006 that the Dutch government would not bring charges against *Jyllands-Posten*. Nonetheless, this episode emphasizes the fact that the debate over insult laws is far from over. What is clear is that a solution to these issues must be found in order for media to be an effective tool in overcoming the Reformers' Dilemma as discussed in Chapter 2. Absent effective checks and balances on government, insult laws will continue to be used to repress dissent and criticism, resulting in a significantly weakened and less effective media.

Reporters Sans Frontières produces an annual press freedom report that tracks the various forms of coercion experienced by journalists and media employees around the world. This provides some insight into the nature and magnitude of coercion faced by journalists. Table 3.2 illustrates the level of coercion by region by showing the total number of journalist killed arrested, attacked, or censored by region for 2007, as well as totals for 2005 and 2006.

The data provided in the report are only for those cases of coercion that can be directly and clearly linked to individuals' work as journalists

Table 3.2   Journalist coercion by region—2007

	Killed	Arrested	Physically attacked or threatened	Media outlets censored
Africa	12	162	145	61
The Americas	7	86	626	91
Asia	17	430	562	273
Europe (including ex-Soviet bloc)	2	77	83	60
North Africa and Middle East	48	132	95	43
2007 Totals	86	887	1511	528
2006 Totals	81	871	1472	912
2005 Totals	63	807	1308	1006

Source: Reporters Sans Frontières 2008 and http://www.rsf.org/article.php3?id_article=24909, accessed 11 January 2009

or media employees. As the data indicate, all of the categories increased over their 2005 and 2006 levels except for media outlets censored, which fell. Arrests are typically made for charges associated with violations of insult laws as discussed above. Censorship usually involves either direct or indirect efforts to close or stifle the reporting of media outlets. In absolute terms, the largest number of journalist arrests in 2007 took place in Asia while the greatest number of physical attacks or threats took place in the Americas. The North Africa and Middle East Region proved to be the most dangerous for journalists. In 2007, 48 journalist/ media employee deaths occurred, over double the amount in any other region.

Also of interest are the trends for these various categories. Has the coercion of journalists and media employees gotten better or worse over time? To provide insight into this question, Figures 3.1 and 3.2 provide global trend data for the number of journalists killed, arrested, and physically attacked or threatened. The trends do not provide reason for optimism. As Figure 3.1 indicates, 2007 was the deadliest year for journalists and media employees since 1994. Further, the number of journalists killed per year has steadily increased since 2002. The trends for both journalist arrests and physical attacks and threats also increased between 1999 and 2006. Such coercion, of course, reduces the ability of journalists to effectively report news and hence weakens media as a source of credible information.

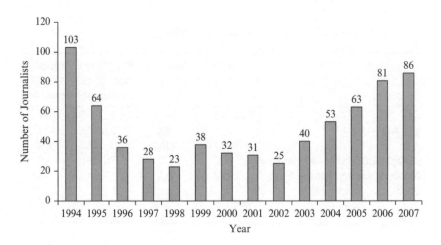

Source: Reporters Sans Frontières 2008

Figure 3.1   Number of journalists killed worldwide—1994–2007

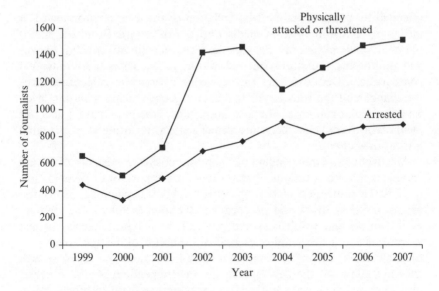

Source: Reporters Sans Frontières 2008

Figure 3.2 Number of journalists arrested and physically attacked or threatened worldwide—1999–2007

The Legal Environment and the Reformers' Dilemma

Basic protections against arrest and physical intimidation and attack are fundamental necessities for the media to provide a solution to the Reformers' Dilemma. Journalists and media employees must be able to report information—critical or otherwise—without the threat of arrest or intimidation. This is the only way that the media can fully serve to check government actions. Further, to the extent that the threat of arrest and intimidation influences the news stories covered, media will suffer from a lack of credibility. Similar to the implications of direct and indirect government manipulation of the media, consumers will discount information if they believe it is biased and inaccurate. The result is that media is weakened as a check on government and as a mechanism of policy and institutional change. When this occurs, the Reformers' Dilemma may persist without a coordination-enhancing device to foster cooperation around good conjectures. The result is that politicians capable of reforms in the interest of the country will instead pursue their private interests.

Further, similar to the case of media manipulation, laws aimed to constrain the media can generate an outcome that is different from that intended by political actors. Manipulation of the legal environment is a means of constraining what media outlets can report. From the standpoint of political actors, this can have the benefit of reducing dissent and reinforcing the status quo. However, it can have the unintended consequence of contributing to the wedge between private preferences for change and the status quo. If this divergence reaches a certain level, a tipping point can ensue. In such an instance, the punctuation effect of media will overwhelm the reinforcement effect, resulting in punctuated institutional change.

An effective and independent media presupposes the existence of certain complementary institutions. Perhaps the most important of these institutions is the protection of basic property rights (for example, protection against physical attack and violence) and the right to voice one's opinion, even if in dissent. Insult laws and physical threats and violence against journalists and media employees weaken the ability of media to overcome the Reformers' Dilemma. Complementary institutions that prevent such coercion allow for the development of an independent media. Further, once in place, an independent media can strengthen these existing complementary institutions by serving as a monitoring device against violations of these rights and so on. This illustrates the potential reinforcement effect of media on existing policies and institutions.

QUALITY OF MEDIA

In April 2003, Jayson Blair resigned from his position as a staff reporter at *The New York Times*. The impetus for Blair's resignation was the revelation that he had plagiarized and fabricated numerous stories that had appeared in print. The Blair case highlights the importance of the quality of media and media reporting. As this case highlights, media quality is an issue even in the most developed of countries and at the most reputable of media outlets. The environment in developing countries is even more difficult in this regard.

The quality of media refers in part to journalistic standards and ethics. It involves the guidelines by which the media industry operates and delivers news stories. Clearly the notions of media independence and media quality are connected. As we discussed in an earlier section, government manipulation of the media can compromise the quality of the news provided to consumers. Likewise, the threat of coercion will influence the quality of the media and the ability of journalists to produce quality news. While media independence deals with the freedom from state ownership and intervention, media quality focuses on standards and training of media employees, as well as the importance of feedback mechanisms that serve to check the behavior of media outlets (Islam 2002: 5).

The problem of media quality in developing countries is perhaps most evident in the difficulty of finding well-trained employees to staff media firms. This difficulty ranges from the business management of the firm, to journalists lacking skills on how to interpret and report information, to editors, analysts, and researchers who are not trained to efficiently and accurately find and analyze information. The lack of training and standards is especially problematic in countries transitioning from planned economies to capitalism. In many countries the culture of corruption and side payments has carried over to the post-communist period, hampering media quality. For example, in Russia in the 1990s, privately-owned media outlets offered favorable coverage to politicians and businessmen in exchange for payments. Such problems, however, are not limited to central and eastern Europe. More recently, for example, accusations of the United States paying reporters in Iraq to publish favorable news stories regarding U.S. military occupation have surfaced (Jervis and Sabah 2005; Mould 2005). These payments hamper the development of an independent media because they foster a culture in which the media is viewed as an uncritical mouthpiece of the state.

As another example of this consider the case of the Philippines. While the media in the Philippines is relatively free, it has suffered from issues of quality as discussed above. For example, in an analysis of the 1998 elections, Chay Florentino-Hofileña (1999) found that reporters were paid monthly bribes by candidates for favorable coverage. This is part of a larger network of journalist and media practitioners identified by Hofileña who are willing to accept bribes for specific stories. This corruption in the media weakens its effectiveness in overcoming the Reformers' Dilemma by reducing the legitimacy of media-provided information.

Even with complete media independence and a stable and favorable legal structure, an inability to accurately gather and report information will greatly weaken the ability of the media to serve as a coordination-enhancing mechanism. It may also lead to the misreporting of information, weakening the media as a means of transparency and potentially coordinating consumers around bad conjectures, as illustrated in the lower right-hand box of the coordination game illustrated in Figure 2.3 (Chapter 2).

Media Quality and the Reformers' Dilemma

No matter what the underlying cause, poor quality curtails the effectiveness of the media as a mechanism for solving the Reformers' Dilemma.

A lack of standards and ethics will lead to a lack of credibility among consumers. A lack of training of journalists and management will threaten the sustainability of independent media outlets because a poorly organized and operated media outlet is less likely to sustain over the long run. There are at least two solutions to the problem of media quality.

The first solution is opening the media market to external influences. For this to be an effective strategy, it requires not only the opening of borders but the prior establishment of a stable legal and property structure such that it is an attractive market for external media sources. Assuming the media market is opened, external influences can occur on several levels. On the one hand, foreign direct investment may serve to overcome the problem of management. Moreover, if foreign journalists, analysts, and researchers are able to work in the domestic media industry, they will bring their skills with them. Additionally, there is always the possibility of learning "on the job" as illustrated by TV-2 in Russia, which has become a thriving media outlet. Those running TV-2 in the 1990s had little knowledge or experience of running a TV station, but through trial and error, along with assistance from foreign consultants, were able to sustain and develop the station (Muchnik and Muchnik 2002: 304–305).

The impact of opening the media industry to outside influences is not limited to those effects outlined above. The very existence of foreign media sources creates an environment of competition, as well as a model for the local media. Foreign media sources—many of which have an established reputation and credibility—serve as a check on the local media against misreporting. They also serve as an additional source of information to the populace, and hence, increase transparency regarding the activities of the government. When *The New York Times*, *The Wall Street Journal* or *The Financial Times* reports a story, it has instant credibility given the track record of these media outlets. For example, in Korea and Russia *The Financial Times* is considered more credible than many of the local news sources (Dyck and Zingales 2002: 120). This forces local media outlets not only to recognize the stories receiving coverage from these major outlets, but also to cover them accurately.

The second solution to the problem of media quality is the establishment of independent press councils. These are autonomous bodies that govern the media industry. Press councils have no legal powers but instead serve a governance function, monitoring the media industry. This monitoring includes interactions between media outlets and political agents, and also the integrity of media outlets themselves. The aim of press council activities is to encourage responsibility on the part of media outlets and protect media freedoms by enforcing a code of conduct and set of standards. Without the ability to legally sanction media outlets, the effectiveness of press councils depends on the cooperation of the relevant groups involved.

Because of its nature as a body of governance, press councils are typically established by members of the media industry. The councils depend on a number of sources for funding, including membership fees and donations from non-profit organizations. Press councils receive complaints about harassment, and false or misreported information, and publicly report on such issues. Further, press councils, at least in principle, are designed to be outside the control of any one political interest.

To illustrate the role of independent press councils, consider the case of Australia, where press freedom is not expressly guaranteed by constitutional means, but rather exists via convention and precedent. A key aspect of the sustainability of the free press is the Australian Press Council.[2] Created in 1976 by publishers and the Australian Journalists Association, the Council protects the rights of journalists to access and report information. It consists of 21 members, including publishers, journalists, members of the public, and an independent chairman. In addition to monitoring the freedoms of journalists, it also accepts and evaluates complaints by journalists against political agents and organizations and also by the public against specific media outlets. The Council will hear complaints against all media that is publicly circulated, even if the outlet producing the media is not a member of the Council. It has no formal authority and no official power of sanction and depends on members cooperating with the Council's guidelines as outlined in its constitution. Finally, the Council tends to address complaints and concerns quickly, especially compared to formal courts.

Of course the emergence of independent press councils requires a specific set of preconditions. Members of the media industry must be willing to participate in the council's founding and cooperate with the guidelines developed. Further, governments must let such independent bodies develop and operate without interference or coercion. Where independent press councils do emerge, they can play a critical role in overcoming problems of media quality by developing and enforcing standards and journalist ethics. Further, by tracking and reporting on instances of journalist harassment and coercion, press councils can potentially play a key role in ensuring that journalists and media employees are protected from the various forms of coercion discussed in the previous section. Where press councils are effective in these roles, they enable media as a potential solution to the Reformers' Dilemma.

There is an important link between media quality and the three effects discussed in Chapter 1. The quality of the information reported will influence the alternative perceptions and ideas presented to consumers, and will therefore impact the gradual effect of media on institutional change.

Likewise, the quality of the information provided will influence the existence of potential tipping points as well as the ability of citizens to activate these tipping points. Recall that punctuated institutional change requires citizens to coordinate their actions to take advantage of potential tipping points. Media can serve this function, but only if the information provided allows citizens to effectively coordinate with others. Finally, to the extent that media is a coordination-enhancing mechanism, the quality of information may impact the way that media reinforces existing institutional equilibria. Poor-quality information may coordinate citizens on bad conjectures and reinforce those conjectures over time.

ECONOMIC FACTORS INFLUENCING MEDIA

The recognition that the media exists within an existing institutional context has a long history. Writing in 1835, Richard Cobden recorded his observations about newspapers in the United States after returning from his travels throughout the country. Cobden calculated that the per capita circulation of newspapers in the United States was six times higher than in the British Isles (Starr 2004: 86). Cobden attributed this difference to the fact that America did not have stamp duties or taxes on paper, ink, and type as Britain did. According to Cobden, these taxes and duties raised the cost of newspapers in the British Isles, stifling the newspaper industry.

Alexis de Tocqueville (1835–1840) also noticed the abundance of papers in America during his travels. While he recognized the importance of minimal regulatory burdens for the growth of newspapers in the United States, Tocqueville offered an additional explanation for the difference in the number of papers in the United States and the British Isles. He attributed the larger number of U.S. newspapers to the structure of the American political system. Specifically, he noted that the decentralized structure of the U.S. political system created a demand for information so that citizens could stay well-informed regarding local and national happenings. In other words, the ability to participate in the political process provided an incentive to citizens to stay informed, which was revealed in their demand for local and national news.

Although different in their emphases, the explanations provided by Cobden and Tocqueville for the abundance of papers in the United States highlight an important point. Economic, political, and social institutions create various incentives for those in the media industry or for those considering entering the industry. In this section we focus on some of the main economic factors that influence media's effectiveness in overcoming the Reformers' Dilemma.

Consumer Demand and Media Content

Like all other firms in a market economy, independent media outlets are subject to the forces of profit and loss. Once state funding is removed, media firms, as agents of consumers, are constrained by consumer demands. Consumer demand for news and information is a function of their income and preferences, the prices of other products, and the size of the market.

Income, along with the prices of goods, determines what consumers can afford to purchase. Wealthier individuals will be able to afford more media products, all other things equal. To the extent that media products are "normal goods"—meaning quantity demanded is positively correlated with income—increases in income will lead to increased demand for more information and news, all else held constant. Preferences or tastes will determine the types of stories and news that media outlets provide to consumers. For example, if enough consumers demand coverage of government corruption or international policy, media sources will adjust their coverage accordingly. Likewise, if consumers demand tabloids and entertainment reporting, media outlets will respond. Typically, as countries and the media market develop and become denser, numerous media outlets develop which specialize in different niches—politics, business, sports, entertainment, and so on. Tastes and preferences need not remain constant. Indeed, while existing preferences determine the types of media coverage provided, media coverage can simultaneously influence and shape consumer preferences. For example, David Throsby (1994) has analyzed how cultural products can be habit forming. His basic argument is that the consumption of cultural products in the present period not only increases utility in the present, but also change tastes due to an accumulation of knowledge and appreciation for the product. This change in tastes makes future consumption of the product that much more enjoyable.

As an example, consider the case of the newspaper *Rzeczpospolita* in Poland. It was owned and operated by the state under the communist regime, but was privatized in 1991. In order to attract readers, *Rzeczpospolita* expanded its economic and political coverage and created the "green pages," which focused specifically on Poland's economic development in terms of the policies political actors adopted as well as their progress. The paper served as a key information source on the mass privatization, allowing readers to realize the benefits and track the progress of political efforts (Carrington and Nelson 2002: 235). Demonstrating the gradual and reinforcement effects, *Rzeczpospolita* shaped consumer preferences and also institutionalized the reforms by creating common knowledge around new policies and institutions.

The price of other goods also influences the demand for media goods. Specifically, within the broad media market, the price of one media product will directly influence the demand for other, substitute, media products. For example, if the price of one media product falls, demand for substitute media products will fall as well. Competition between media products is therefore an important factor influencing the demand for them. The process of competition tends to cause prices to fall over time, which will tend to increase the quantity of media products demanded, all else held constant.

As a specific example of the impact of competition on demand, consider the case of India. The circulation of major newspapers in India increased approximately 13 per cent between 2005 and 2007. A driving factor behind this growth is increased competition between newspapers. The *Times of India* has started a trend where established regional papers expand to compete in the national market. This has forced papers to increase the diversity of topics covered in order to attract the broadest audience possible. Moreover, the increased competition has led papers to offer deep subscription discounts to consumers. The falling subscription prices, in turn, mean that more consumers can afford to subscribe to a daily newspaper (*Economist* 2007a). Finally, the size of the market (that is, the number of potential buyers) also plays a role in the demand for media products. All else held constant, the larger the number of potential buyers, the greater the demand for media products.[3]

Consumer demand, and the factors that influence demand, are critical for the effectiveness of the media as a solution to the Reformers' Dilemma. Even if the factors discussed in previous sections—government intervention in the media industry, the legal environment and media quality—are favorable, consumers must demand certain information for the media to be an effective means of transforming the initial situation of conflict into a situation of coordination according to the Reformers' Dilemma model. Consumer demand for information regarding reforms is critical to this process because it puts pressure on those in positions of political power who can influence the reform process. In other words, the demand for information regarding politicians' activities is correlated with media monitoring. Further, as consumers demand information and media outlets respond, that information and the expectation of future reporting on the topic become institutionalized.

It is important to note that consumer demand, though it may very well keep media sources in business, does not guarantee the successful adoption of policies and institutions conducive to economic development. Assuming that media is an effective coordination mechanism, the populace and reformers must coordinate around good conjectures. If politicians carry out the wishes of the populace but the demands are for policies and institutions that are bad for economic development, growth will not be achieved. In short, successful development requires that, in addition to the factors outlined above, indigenous conjectures, ideas and demands align with policies and institutions that promote economic growth. If the populace and politicians coordinate on bad conjectures, economic development may fail to occur despite a free media.

As per the "reinforcement effect," the media may also strengthen existing conjectures, good or bad. As highlighted in the previous section on media quality, if there is misreporting of information, the media may coordinate consumers around bad policies. In the introductory chapter we discussed the process of institutional change and how it entails shifts in underlying perceptions and belief systems. We also discussed the importance of institutional "path dependency," which emphasizes that past experiences and beliefs constrain the set of feasible choices in the current period. Along these lines, research indicates that there is a tendency for journalists to accept the ideologies that are dominant in the societies they work in and hence strengthen that dominant view (Epstein 1973; Gans 1979; Sahr 1993). This is a double-edged sword. To the extent that the media has this reinforcing effect on ideology, those that initially coordinate on good conjectures may develop more rapidly, while it may be more difficult for those that coordinate on bad conjectures to switch course. In addition to being free from government interference and facing a favorable legal structure, the effectiveness of media in coordination scenarios requires quality reporting and consumer demand for policies that lead to economic development.

It is also important to note that there is an important relationship between the health of the media industry and the economy in general. For example, Carrington and Nelson (2002: 229–230) show a positive correlation between media strength—measured by media reach and independence—and economic health—measured by a mix of 21 variables including per capita GDP, debt levels, and trade. In many cases, media firms face the negative economic situation that characterizes developing countries. In such instances, the stagnation of the general economic environment puts pressure on the media industry, resulting in outlets going out of business or turning to the state for support. Belarus and Zimbabwe are two examples of this. In both cases, general economic hardship resulted in reductions in press independence and freedom (Carrington and Nelson 2002: 229–230). When this occurs, the independence and sustainability of media is limited, as is its ability to increase transparency and serve as a coordination-enhancing mechanism around policy and institutional change.

Advertising

Advertising is a critical aspect of a free media. Revenue in the media industry typically comes from two sources—subscriptions and advertising. In most media markets, advertising is the main source of revenue. In lower-income countries, where the broader economy is still developing, a lack of private advertising expenditures can pose a major problem for media outlets. Given the importance of this factor, we dedicate a separate sub-section to a discussion of the importance of advertising and the factors that influence it.

In the context of media, advertising involves the sale of a captive audience to other producers. The economic explanation for advertising deals with overcoming problems related to asymmetric information. Advertising serves the critical role of informing consumer of goods and services and influencing their tastes for such goods. In this sense, advertising facilitates the interaction between buyers and sellers by reducing transaction costs (see Ekelund and Saurman 1988). The types of advertising offered by media outlets vary from specific content printed in newspapers to commercial broadcasts on television and radio to pop-up ads on websites.

The success of media outlets in developing countries will be largely dependent on the existence and robustness of advertising revenue. As such, the general economic environment, as well as government policies toward both media outlets and businesses in general, will influence the level of advertising. Figure 3.3 shows the growth of total advertising expenditures for several transition countries. As the figure indicates, total advertising expenditure in Poland, Hungary, Slovenia, and the Czech Republic grew by several multiples over the 1994–2000 period. These countries are included in the list of successful transition countries that adopted sustainable market-based reforms. These reforms contributed to an environment conducive to the growth of private industry, which in turn contributed to the growth of advertising expenditures. Each of these countries also adopted reforms to free the media from government control. The growth of advertising revenues allowed the independent media to sustain and reform.

Russia stands in stark contrast to these other transition countries considered. While total advertising revenues did increase during the 1994–2000 period, the increase was a significantly smaller amount than that of the other transition countries. This relatively small growth reflects the general economic conditions of Russia as well as continued government involvement in the media industry. During 1990–1999, Russia's GDP experienced an average decline of 6.1per cent (Carrington and Nelson 2002: 237). The financial crisis in 1998 also severely hampered the advertising market,

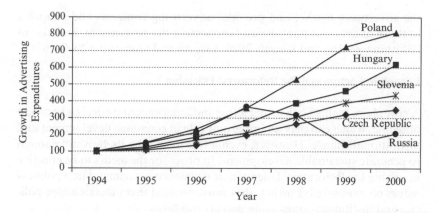

Note: Index, 1994 = 100.

Source: Carrington and Nelson 2002: 236

*Figure 3.3   Advertising expenditure growth, selected transition countries,
1994–2000*

among many others. Moreover, the government continued to remain
involved in the media. In many cases the state provided direct subsidies
to the media, which weakened the need to generate private advertising
revenue to stay in business. The combination of economic downturns and
government subsidies slowed the growth in the advertising market, as well
as the sustainability of the independent press.

As important as the size of advertising revenue for media independence, and thus media's ability to overcome the Reformers' Dilemma, is the
source of this revenue. In many developing countries, the advertising sector
is dominated by government-purchased advertisements (Carrington and
Nelson 2002: 228–229). This dependency on state revenue can result in the
manipulation of the media by the government. In Romania, for example,
many private media outlets rely heavily upon state-purchased advertisements to remain in business. The government often uses this financial
power to pressure media sources to bias reported information such that
it favors the governing party. The State Ownership Fund (FPS) decides
which media outlets various state-owned enterprises will contract with
for advertisements. As a government institution, the FPS is able to effectively wield this power to influence media sources in need of advertisement
revenue. For instance, the FPS may agree to purchase advertising space
in a newspaper if the newspaper agrees to favor the governing party in its
coverage. A similar situation exists in Nepal, where government dominates

the advertising market and provides advertising contracts and subsidies to those outlets that publish news supporting the government, and also in Pakistan (see Rao and Koirala 2000: 138; Ali and Gunaratne 2000: 167).

Economic Factors and the Reformers' Dilemma

A core claim in this book is that a free and independent media is a first-best outcome, which can play an important role in economic development and institutional change. However, even a free media, by itself, is not enough to generate sustainable development. In order for the media to be effective in solving the Reformers' Dilemma, consumers must demand that political actors be monitored. Further, they must demand that officials adopt policies and institutions supporting good conjectures.

We emphasized that the media in developing countries is subject to general economic conditions, as well as the existence or absence of advertising markets and associated revenue. Advertising revenue is critical to the independence and sustainability of an independent media. How then are developing countries to handle the problems of economic instability and underdeveloped advertising markets? Government subsidies and advertising contracts are a poor solution. As discussed in this section, as well as the earlier section on government manipulation of the media, government subsidies and advertising contracts erode the independence of the media and allow government officials to capture the media to serve their own private interests. This has the effect of diminishing the credibility and effectiveness of the media as a monitoring device. This outcome is even more likely in developing countries where checks and balances on government interventions are fragile or non-existent.

An alternative solution is the opening of a country's borders to foreign investment in the media industry. Such a policy expands the media and advertising markets beyond the underdeveloped domestic markets to include the markets in other, more developed, countries. To provide a concrete example of this solution, it is useful to return again to the case of *Rzeczpospolita* in Poland. Recall that it was cut off from state funding upon its privatization in 1991. Facing undeveloped advertising markets to sustain itself financially, it relied on foreign investment for its survival. The France-based Hersant newspaper group purchased 49 per cent of *Rzeczpospolita* in 1991 and used its own resources to upgrade the paper's technology (Carrington and Nelson 2002: 235). The initial investment allowed *Rzeczpospolita* to continue in operation and develop a customer base while Poland's advertising market developed. As discussed above, the paper eventually expanded its coverage and has become one of the most popular papers in Poland.

The case of *Rzeczpospolita* provides a blueprint for how developing countries should address the issues discussed in this section. By creating an environment conducive to foreign investment, developing countries can provide an incentive for foreign investors to commit resources to the development of the domestic media. This again highlights the importance of complementary institutions for the development and sustainability of an independent press. Institutions such as the protection of property rights, favorable taxes and regulations, and an effective process for dispute resolution will foster foreign investment, which will contribute to an independent press, among other industries.

It is also important to reiterate the importance of the dual role of media in policy and institutional change (see Chapter 1). The media can serve to coordinate citizens on specific policies within a given set of institutions. This includes the initial adoption of policies, as well as the reinforcement of those policies over time. At the same time, the media can serve as a catalyst of gradual and punctuated institutional change. In this regard the media can contribute to the process of bringing about fundamental changes in institutions.

Recognizing these dual roles provides some insight into the "chicken or egg" paradox associated with the role of a media in adopting policies and institutions conducive to development. On the one hand a flourishing independent media requires the aforementioned complementary institutions. On the other hand it is unclear how these complementary institutions emerge in the first place. In other words, how do institutions enabling an independent media emerge absent an independent media? The answer to this question is that media, even where initially unfree, can contribute to the evolution of the complementary institutions necessary for an independent media.

For example, an underground press might develop which disseminates alternative information, views, and perceptions. Once the process is in motion it is possible for complementary institutions to emerge which nourish the subsequent growth of an independent press. As our case studies will detail, in Poland and Russia an illegal underground media played a key role in initiating broader institutional changes which led to subsequent policy and institutions. In these cases, media served as an initial catalyst of change despite the fact that it was largely unfree.

SUMMATION

This chapter has discussed and analyzed several of the key factors influencing the effectiveness of the media as a mechanism for solving the

Reformers' Dilemma. A number of important themes and implications stem from this analysis.

Our discussion of government media manipulation has three primary implications. First, indirect control of media is just as important, if not more so, than direct state ownership in determining government's ability to manipulate media-provided information. Indeed, three of the four methods of state media manipulation considered—financial pressure, infrastructure control, and entry regulation—are indirect in nature and consistent with privately owned media outlets. Thus the presence of private media outlets is far from sufficient to establish media independence. Even where media infrastructure is privately owned, if government can financially pressure media outlets and infrastructure owners in the ways described above, or can restrict entry into these industries, its ability to manipulate media-provided information remains strong.

Second, the general regulatory and tax environment of a country is critical to government's ability to manipulate the media. Where regulations are costly, numerous, ambiguous, and change frequently, those in power can use the guise of regulatory infractions to financially and/or operationally choke media outlets and infrastructure owners who refuse to bias reporting or to remain silent on issues that reflect poorly on those in power. Additionally, an onerous and ambiguous regulatory environment empowers politicians to blackmail media outlets to do their bidding with the threat of infraction or by obtaining sensitive information the government can use to cut off an outlet's main sources of revenue. Similarly, if taxation is sufficiently high, government can drive media sources into state debt and then use this as leverage to control the content of media reporting.

Third, the public's perception about media's credibility is crucial to its ability to affect positive reform. Where media is dependent upon government, media-provided information is not perceived as credible in the minds of citizens. Knowing that information is incomplete and inaccurate, citizens discount this information and have greater difficulty making political decisions that correspond to politicians' pursuit of public or privately interested policies and institutions. In other words, citizens find it more difficult to effectively monitor political agents. As a result, politicians who pursue privately interested policy may not be forced to change or be rooted out and replaced with those who pursue publicly interested policy. Furthermore, with the knowledge that citizens cannot rely upon media-provided information to monitor them, self-interested politicians are encouraged to make policies that benefit a small segment of society at the expense of everyone else. The absence of media credibility also weakens its ability to institutionalize reforms and changes for the better because of the lack of legitimacy among consumers. Consumers will discount the publicly reported information and will suffer from coordination failure because they cannot be sure how other consumers interpret and discount this information. An underground media can help to overcome the credibility crises created by government manipulation of official media. But precisely because these media are underground, the task is more difficult.

Additionally, our analysis points to an important, if obvious, conclusion concerning threats against media industry employees and the effectiveness of the media in overcoming the Reformers' Dilemma. Journalists and other media employees must be protected from physical coercion in order to be effective in their jobs. Developing countries must take steps to protect journalists and media employees in this regard. Less obvious is how to deal with the problems associated with indirect coercion in the form of insult laws and arrests for violating those laws. Recall that insult laws refer to regulations that make it illegal to criticize certain government officials or members of the ruling elite. The ideal strategy for developing countries is to repeal insult laws and completely remove them from the books. The problem with attempting to revise and reword existing insult laws is that they leave open the possibility that these laws can be abused in the future. This is especially important in developing countries where the checks and balances on government officials are weak. The long-term robustness of the system requires abolishing laws, like insult laws, that allow for arbitrary accusations by political leaders.

Walden (2002: 216–217) contends that criminal penalties for libel and slander should also be abolished. She contends that issues of defamation should be handled within the realm of civil law instead of criminal law. Further, standards must be put in place for determining guilt in such cases. Simple allegations by members of the political elite should not be sufficient to produce a guilty verdict. Instead, the plaintiffs should have the obligation of demonstrating that the claims being made are false.

Our analysis of media quality and the economic determinants of media effectiveness has important implications for establishing and maintaining an independent media. In many developing countries, media employees lack training and journalistic standards and ethics are either lacking or absent. Further, private markets are underdeveloped, making it difficult for private media outlets to sustain. One immediate solution to this problem is to allow foreign investment and ownership of domestic media outlets. In many cases, foreign investors and owners will provide financial support that allows media outlets to develop. The opening of borders also allows developing countries to import journalistic standards and ethics, as well as management capabilities that already exist in other countries. Empirical studies support the importance of foreign ownership for good political outcomes (Besley and Prat 2006). In addition to providing financial support, training, and standards to media outlets in developing countries, foreign owners will also tend to be more insulated from government attempts to manipulate the media. As such, foreign ownership is yet another means of strengthening media as a check on government actions.

Our discussion of consumer demand highlights the importance of consumer sovereignty. Ultimately, a free and independent press requires the recognition that consumers determine what information is supplied in the media market. At some point the demand for certain types of news products and reporting may be low or non-existent. In some cases this may lead to a call for government subsidies to provide either alternative forms of media or alternative reporting not currently demanded by consumers. However, government subsidies of this sort again open up the real possibility of government manipulation of the media that this chapter has discussed. Given this, government subsidies of any form—direct subsidies, advertising contracts, partial ownership or partnering and so on—should not be viewed as a viable alternative. On the contrary, state support is likely to exacerbate the lack of media freedom rather than improve this situation.

A free media does not guarantee a solution to the Reformers' Dilemma. It is an important, but not sufficient, condition for economic development. Consumers must demand certain reforms and behaviors from officials. They must also demand certain media coverage of those behaviors. Where such demand is weak or non-existent, the solution is not state intervention in the media. Such a policy is an open invitation for government manipulation of the media and the stagnation of reforms conducive to liberal institutions. This is especially the case in developing countries where checks and balances on government are weak or non-existent. It is also important to note that consumer demands can change over time and that entrepreneurs in the media industry play a key role in influencing and shaping those demands, as the example of *Rzeczpospolita* discussed earlier highlighted.

Governments set the formal rules of the game within which economic interactions take place. These rules provide incentives to engage in certain kinds of behaviors by influencing the relative payoffs associated with various courses of action. In the context of media, the goal of governments in developing countries should be to create a set of rules conducive to creating an independent and sustainable press. The first-best outcome entails privatizing all aspects of the media industry and removing all government connections to it. This includes government connections to primary media outlets but also to the infrastructure that supports media outlets. Government subsidies should be reduced to zero as quickly as possible to avoid backsliding and government manipulation in future periods.

Rules must be established that protect journalists from coercion or the threat thereof. Finally, an environment conducive to foreign investment and ownership in the media industry must be established. This includes removing trade barriers, minimal taxation and regulation and the effective protection of property and contracts. Laws aimed at "cultural protection" which outlaw, or severely limit, exchange in cultural products with other countries should be removed to allow the free flow of resources and ideas. These outcomes are the ideal. In reality, any step toward this goal is preferable to the status quo.

One problem with many of the changes recommended here to improve the media's effectiveness in overcoming the Reformers' Dilemma is that, to achieve them, at least a partial solution to the Reformers' Dilemma may be required to begin with. Recognizing the dual role of media, as well as the three effects of media on policies and institutions, sheds light on a solution to this apparent paradox. The media does not have to be initially free to generate policy and institutional changes leading to subsequent changes. Even where media is largely unfree, there are other sources of information—underground media, foreign media, think tanks, government watchdog groups, academics, political campaigns, and so on—which provide citizens with alternative ideas and information. This alternative information can contribute to a divergence between private preferences for changes and the status quo. When this "preference gap" reaches a tipping point, dramatic punctuated change is possible. The media can serve an important role, not only in disseminating information that contributes to the formation of the preference gap, but also in coordinating people around a new punctuated equilibrium. In such an instance, even a relatively unfree media can generate change for the better.

ACKNOWLEDGEMENTS

This chapter draws from parts of Coyne and Leeson (2004) and Leeson and Coyne (2005).

NOTES

1. Pre-1997, media received preferential tax treatment. Media products had the lowest VAT in Romania.
2. Australian Press Council website: http://www.presscouncil.org.au.
3. Note that when all other factors are not held constant, the size of the market, as measured by population, is not a suitable indicator of consumer demand for media products. For example, the demand for media products is larger in the United States as compared

to China and India, which have much larger populations. This is due to differences in levels of income in these countries. While the populations of China and India are significantly larger than that of the United States, per capita income in the U.S. is significantly higher, offsetting the effects of population differences (Hoskins, McFadyen and Finn 2004: 46).

REFERENCES

Ali, Owais Aslam and Shelton A. Gunaratne (2000) "Pakistan." In Shelton A. Gunaratne (ed.), *Handbook of the Media in Asia*. New Delhi: Sage Publications, pp. 155–181.

Banisar, David (2006). *Freedom of Information Around the World 2006*. London: Privacy International.

Besley, Timothy and Robin Burgess (2002) "The Political Economy of Government Responsiveness: Theory and Evidence from India," *Quarterly Journal of Economics*, 117: 1415–1452.

Besley, Timothy and Andrea Prat (2006) "Handcuffs for the Grabbing Hand? Media Capture and Government Accountability," *American Economic Review*, 96: 720–736.

Carrington, Tim and Mark Nelson (2002) 'Media in Transition: The Hegemony of Economics'. In Alisa Clapp-Itnyre, Roumeen Islam and Caralee McLiesh (eds), *The Right to Tell: The Role of Mass Media in Economic Development*. Washington DC: The World Bank, pp. 225–248.

Coyne, Christopher and Peter Leeson (2004) "Read All About It! Understanding the Role of Media in Economic Development," *Kyklos*, 57: 21–44.

Djankov, Simeon, Caralee McLiesh, Tatiana Nenova, and Andrei Shleifer (2003) "Who Owns the Media?" *Journal of Law and Economics*, 46: 341–382.

Dyck, Alexander and Luigi Zingales (2002) 'The Corporate Governance Role of the Media'. In Alisa Clapp-Itnyre, Roumeen Islam and Caralee McLiesh (eds), *The Right to Tell: The Role of Mass Media in Economic Development*. Washington DC: The World Bank, pp. 107–140.

Economist (2007a) "Let 1,000 Titles Bloom," *The Economist*, 17 February: 69.

Economist (2007b) "An Opposition Gagged," *The Economist*, 2 June: 38–39.

Ekelund, Jr, Robert B. and Daniel S. Saurman (1988) *Advertising and the Market Process*. San Francisco, CA: Pacific Research Institute.

Epstein, Edward J. (1973) *News From Nowhere: Television and the News*. New York: Vintage.

Florentino-Hofileña, Chay (1999) *News for Sale: The Corruption of the Philippine Media*. Manila: Philippine Center for Investigative Journalism.

Frank, Leonard Roy (2003) *Freedom*. New York: Random House.

Freedom House (2003) *Freedom of the Press 2003: A Global Survey of Media Independence*. New York: Rowman and Littlefield Publishers, Inc.

Gans, Herbert (1979) *Deciding What's News*. New York: Vintage.

Greene, Marilyn (ed.) (2006) *It's a Crime: How Insult Laws Stifle Press Freedom*. Reston, VA: World Press Freedom Committee.

Grossman, Sanford and Oliver Hart (1986) "The Costs and Benefits of Ownership: A Theory of Vertical and Lateral Integration," *Journal of Political Economy*, 94: 691–719.

Heo, Chul, Ki-Yul Uhm and Jeong-Heon Chang (2000) "South Korea." In Shelton A. Gunaratne (ed.), *Handbook of the Media in Asia*. New Delhi: Sage Publications, pp. 611–637.

Hoskins, Colin, Stuart McFadyen and Adam Finn (2004) *Media Economics: Applying Economics to New and Traditional Media*. Thousand Oaks, CA: Sage Publications.

International Research and Exchange Board (IREX) (2002) *Media Sustainability Index*. Washington, DC: IREX.

Islam, Roumeen (2002) 'Into the Looking Glass: What the Media Tell and Why – An Overview'. In Alisa Clapp-Itnyre, Roumeen Islam and Caralee McLiesh (eds), *The Right to Tell: The Role of Mass Media in Economic Development*. Washington DC: The World Bank, pp. 1–23.

Jervis, Rick and Zaid Sabah (2005) "Probe into Iraq coverage widens," *USA Today*, 9 December: 1.

Krug, Peter and Monroe E. Price (2002) 'The Legal Environment for News Media'. In Alisa Clapp-Itnyre, Roumeen Islam and Caralee McLiesh (eds), *The Right to Tell: The Role of Mass Media in Economic Development*. Washington DC: The World Bank, pp. 187–206.

Leeson, Peter T. and Christopher J. Coyne (2005) "Manipulating the Media," *Institutions and Economic Development*, 1–2: 67–92.

Liebling, A.J. (1960) "Do You Belong in Journalism?" *New Yorker*, 4 May: 105–112.

Maslog, Crispin C. (2000) "Philippines." In Shelton A. Gunaratne (ed.), *Handbook of the Media in Asia*. New Delhi: Sage Publications, pp. 372–401.

Media Monitoring Agency (2004) *Press Freedom in Romania: Report on 2003*. Bucharest: Media Monitoring Agency Academia.

Mould, David (2005) "Buying News in Iraq," *Global Beat Syndicate*, 13 December, published online, http://www.bu.edu/globalbeat/syndicate/mould121305.html, accessed 11 January 2009.

Muchnik, Viktor and Yulia Muchnik (2002) 'The Survival of a Provincial Television Station in an Era of Enormous Change'. In Alisa Clapp-Itnyre, Roumeen Islam and Caralee McLiesh (eds), *The Right to Tell: The Role of Mass Media in Economic Development*. Washington DC: The World Bank, pp. 301–308.

Panol, Zeny Sarabia and Yen Do (2000) "Vietnam." In Shelton A. Gunaratne (ed.), *Handbook of the Media in Asia*. New Delhi: Sage Publications, pp. 463–486.

Rao, Sandhya and Bharat Koirala (2000) "Nepal." In Shelton A. Gunaratne (ed.), *Handbook of the Media in Asia*. New Delhi: Sage Publications, pp. 132–154.

Reporters Sans Frontières (2008) *Press Freedom in 2008*. Paris: Reporters Sans Frontières.

Romanian Academic Society (2004) "Policy Warning and Forecast Report: Romania in 2004," Bucharest: Romanian Academic Society.

Sahr, Robert (1993) "Credentialing Experts: The Climate of Opinion and Journalist Selection of Sources in Domestic and Foreign Opinion," In Robert Spitzer (ed.), *Media and Public Policy*. Westport, CT: Praeger, 153–170.

Starr, Paul (2004) *The Creation of the Media*. New York: Basic Books.

Throsby, David (1994) "The Production and Consumption of the Arts: A View of Cultural Economics," *Journal of Economic Literature*, 23(1): 1–29.

Tocqueville, Alexis de (1835–1840 [1988]) *Democracy in America*. New York: Harper Perennial.

Walden, Ruth (2002) 'Insult Laws'. In Alisa Clapp-Itnyre, Roumeen Islam and Caralee McLiesh (eds), *The Right to Tell: The Role of Mass Media in Economic Development*. Washington DC: The World Bank, pp. 207–324.

Wang, Georgette and Ven-Hwei Lo (2000) "Taiwan." In Shelton A. Gunaratne (ed.), *Handbook of the Media in Asia*. New Delhi: Sage Publications, pp. 660–681.

4. Inside the black box: media freedom, political knowledge, and participation

INTRODUCTION

A central argument in this book is that a free and independent media is a first-best solution to the Reformers' Dilemma. An independent media provides an incentive for government actors to adopt beneficial reforms instead of focusing on their own narrow interests. The underlying logic is that a free media provides critical information to citizens regarding current events and political activities. As long as there is some political competition, politicians that fail to satisfy citizens' desires will be punished by citizens. A free media serves as a source of knowledge of political activities, and a source of knowledge of other individuals' knowledge of these activities, so that citizens can evaluate politicians and reward or punish them accordingly.

As we discussed in Chapter 1, although democracy is not required for media to help check political actors' behavior, media's ability to perform this function and thus to facilitate policy and institutional change is much stronger when political competition is stronger. By giving people the power to punish politicians at the voting booth, democracy provides citizens with a straightforward and low cost way to use the information the media provides them to punish politicians who do not serve their interests and to reward those who do. In this chapter we focus specifically on media's role in an environment of democratic political competition where citizens can use the voting booth to affect policy and institutional change.

As Chapter 1 discussed, the existing literature exploring the relationship between media and economic development can be broken down into two general categories. The first category explores the media as a mechanism for overcoming the principal–agent problem that citizens confront vis-à-vis their political rulers (see Sen 1984, 1999; Besley and Burgess 2002; Coyne and Leeson 2004; Stromberg 2004; Besley and Prat 2006).[1] This work emphasizes that to effectively monitor politicians and hold unscrupulous ones accountable, citizens must be knowledgeable of at least some basic political facts and issues. Snyder and Stromberg (2004), for instance, find that where voters are better politically informed as a result of more media coverage, politicians are more responsive to their wants.

The second category of research considers how patterns of media ownership affect economic development. This work is typified by Djankov *et al.* (2003), who find that private media ownership is associated with improved social outcomes. In contrast, where the media is state owned, citizens lead poorer, unhealthier, and shorter lives.

Existing research thus establishes the importance of media-provided information in holding political agents accountable on the one hand, and a strong association between media freedom and social outcomes on the other. However, a "black box" remains surrounding the precise nature of the channel that links media, information, and development discussed in the existing literature and in previous chapters of this book. This chapter fills this gap by econometrically examining the relationship between media freedom, citizens' political knowledge, and their political activeness. Our analysis finds a large, positive, and highly significant association between media freedom, political knowledge, political participation, and voter turnout. Where government owns a larger share of media outlets and infrastructure, regulates the media industry more, and does more to control the content of news, citizens are more politically ignorant and apathetic. Where the media is less regulated and there is greater private ownership in the media industry, citizens are more politically knowledgeable and active. This is true even after controlling for a number of factors including income, age, education, and democracy/autocracy.

In light of the existing research discussed above, these findings suggest the following specific channel connecting media and development: in countries where government interferes with the media, individuals know less about basic political issues and are less politically involved. Because they know less about political happenings and participate less politically, they are less effective in monitoring and punishing the activities of self-interested politicians. With less accountability to voters, politicians more frequently pursue privately beneficial policies at the expense of society. This in turn leads to lower development.

The recent transition experience of the post-socialist world provides an excellent ground to explore this channel. Since 1991, the countries of Eastern and Central Europe have moved in different directions with respect to government's relationship to the media. Some, such as Poland, have liberalized substantial portions of their economies, including the media, which used to be in the state's hands. Others, such as Romania, have liberalized comparatively little. In these places the media remains largely under government control. These divergent paths have created interesting variation to exploit for investigating the relationship between media freedom and citizens' political knowledge and participation.

To do this we use data from the 2003 Candidate Countries Eurobarometer survey, which provides information about Eastern and Central Europeans' political knowledge. The Eurobarometer quizzed over 12 000 respondents from 13 Central and Eastern European candidate countries to the European Union on basic political facts about the EU. The EU is an important part of the fabric of European life, so if media freedom is connected to citizens' political knowledge, questions about the EU are a good place to look. Although EU issues are somewhat different from purely local ones, they play a significant role in shaping policies at the local level in EU member and member-bound countries. Measuring citizens' knowledge about basic political facts related to the EU in EU candidate countries therefore measures an important part of their political knowledge, and likely proxies for knowledge about more purely local political issues, which cannot be directly measured through the Eurobarometer quiz.

We search for additional support for the channel connecting media freedom and citizens' political knowledge by exploring the relationship between media freedom and political participation and voter turnout. The reason we look here for support is straightforward. A sizeable literature confirms that where citizens are less politically knowledgeable, they are less likely to vote or otherwise be active in politics. Where they are more knowledgeable, they vote and participate more (see for instance Klingemann 1979; Chong, McClosky and Zaller 1983; Luskin 1990; Junn 1991; Leighley 1991; Zaller 1992; Flanigan and Zingale 1994; Prat and Stromberg 2005). Politically ignorant individuals know less about what they can or should get involved with, find it more difficult to get interested in issues they know little or nothing about, and have less incentive to participate politically since they are less likely to be able to effect change through such action in the first place.

In other words, the underlying source of variation in citizens' political knowledge and participation is largely the same. The relationship between media freedom and political knowledge should therefore parallel its relationship to political participation and voter turnout. If low media freedom is meaningfully associated with political ignorance, we should also find political apathy where the media is less free and vice versa. In addition to establishing the link between media freedom and political participation and voter turnout, an important endeavor in its own right, "triangulating" the evidence this way allows us to strengthen (if a correspondence is found) or weaken (if it is not) our confidence in any relationship discovered between media freedom and political knowledge.

To establish the connection between media freedom and political participation and voter turnout, we draw on two sources. Data from the 1992–2002 wave of the World Values Survey (WVS) (ICPSR 2005) allows us to get at the issue of how media freedom is related to political participation and, following the logic above, indirectly, political knowledge. In addition to the countries covered by the Eurobarometer survey, the WVS contains information on the political participation of more than 50 other nations around the globe. The International Institute for Democracy and Electoral Assistance (2005) provides data for these same 60 or so countries on voter turnout. These data allow us to see how media's relationship to the state might be associated with voter turnout, and again indirectly provide evidence about the connection between media freedom and political knowledge.

Although there is an extensive body of research that examines the determinants of political knowledge, participation, and voter turnout, research investigating the relationship between media freedom and these variables is lacking.[2] Taken together, the evidence suggests that low media freedom is strongly connected to political ignorance and apathy. Like Djankov *et al.* (2003), since we have only a cross-section of countries, this evidence cannot be decisively interpreted as causal. Unmeasured factors may partially account for the observed relationships here, and in the absence of instrumental variables, it is important to bear in mind that in addition to the media freedom impacting political knowledge and participation, these factors may also influence the extent of media freedom in a country. Nevertheless, our analysis provides important evidence on a critical intermediate channel connecting media and development.

Our analysis is structured as followed. We first describe the data used for each set of regressions (political knowledge, political participation, and voter turnout). We then present our benchmark results examining the relationship between media freedom and political knowledge. This is followed by an analysis of the relationship between media freedom and political participation and then a consideration of the connection between media freedom and voter turnout. Finally, we perform some sensitivity analyses and discuss the implications of our analysis.

DATA

Political Knowledge

We use several sources for the data in our regressions that look at the relationship between media freedom and citizen knowledge. Data for our regressand (a citizen's EU quiz score) are from the European Commission's

Candidate Countries Eurobarometer 2003.4 (ICPR 2004), which compiles information from standardized surveys administered to citizens in candidate countries for the European Union. Surveys contain questions relating to citizens' opinions and perceptions of the EU, their knowledge of basic facts about and around the EU, and others.

We are interested in the data relating to respondents' knowledge about the EU since they allow us to objectively determine how knowledgeable citizens are of some basic political facts related to their nation. For instance, one question asks respondents whether or not the President of the EU is directly elected by all the citizens. Another asks if the European flag is bright blue with yellow stars or not. All of the questions have a "true or false" format.[3]

A significant advantage of these questions is that the correct answers are identical for all respondents, regardless of country. Domestic-based political questions, like "What is your President's name?" which have different answers depending upon a respondent's citizenship, do not provide as clean measures of political knowledge. Some rulers are more well-known then others, for instance because they are more charismatic, or associated with infamous scandals. Citizens in these countries are more likely to be able to name their leader regardless of media freedom in their country, and controlling for these factors would be nearly impossible. The questions we use avoid these problems since their correct answers are not domestically dependent.

The Eurobarometer survey was administered in October–November 2003. It covers 13 countries, which at the time of the survey were each candidates to the EU: Bulgaria, Cyprus, the Czech Republic, Estonia, Hungary, Latvia, Lithuania, Malta,[4] Poland, Romania, Slovakia, Slovenia and Turkey. The same set of questions was asked of representative samples of the population aged 15 years and over in each country. Respondents who answered "Don't Know" to a question on the political quiz were scored as having answered this question incorrectly. Those who refused to answer a question were dropped from the dataset, creating a total of 12 006 observations. The sample size for each country was roughly equal (about 1000) with the exception of Malta and Cyprus, which had 500 each.

Data for our variable of interest, media freedom, come from two sources. The first is from Freedom House (2004), which assigns points to countries on the basis of three equally weighted categories related to media's independence from government to create a composite score of media freedom ranging from zero (completely unfree) to one (completely free). These categories are: legal environment, which looks at laws, statutes, constitutional provisions, and regulations that enable or restrict the media's ability to operate freely in a country; political environment, which evaluates the degree of political control over the content of news media in each country (such as editorial independence, official or unofficial censorship, harassment or attacks against journalists); and economic environment, which includes the structure of media ownership, media-related infrastructure, its concentration, the impact of corruption or bribery on news media content, and the selective withholding or bestowal of subsidies or other sources of financial revenue on some media outlets by the state. Media considered by this index include TV, radio, newspaper, and the Internet. Freedom House's measure of media freedom is our benchmark measure. It is the most comprehensive, systematic, and widely-used measure of media freedom, and therefore the most reliable.

As a robustness check, we also consider a second measure of media freedom, which uses a different methodology for arriving at press freedom scores. This measure comes from Reporters Sans Frontières (2003). Its scores are based on a questionnaire with 52 criteria for assessing the degree of media freedom, which include any type of action taken by the government in a country to restrict the independence of journalists or media outlets. These actions include murders, imprisonments, physical attacks or threats against journalists, censorship of media outlets, confiscation, searches, and harassment. The Reporters Sans Frontières scores also take account of the extent of media-related state ownership in each country, the extent of media regulation, and laws punishing free speech including on the Internet. This questionnaire was sent to the organization's 130 correspondents around the world, as well as journalists, researchers, jurists, and human rights activists, to evaluate media freedom in each country for each of these criteria. Media considered by this index again include TV, radio, newspaper, and the Internet. The resulting composite score in each country ranges from zero (completely unfree) to one (completely free). We report our results using the Reporters Sans Frontières measure along with a third measure of media freedom described later in this chapter in our tables that describe sensitivity analyses.

Data for our control variables come from several sources. Data on public expenditures on education (as a percentage of GDP) and GNI (Gross National Income) per capita are from the World Bank's *World Development Indicators* (2004). For the former, we use data from 2003 or the closest available year when data for 2003 are unavailable. For GNI per capita, we use data from 2000. Numbers for educational attainment are from the 2003 Eurobarometer survey, which asks each respondent the age at which they stopped full-time education. The Eurobarometer also provides data on respondent age, income, the amount of TV, daily paper and radio news they consume, and how much attention they pay to the EU. Finally, we obtain data for the degree of democracy/autocracy in each country in 2000 from the Polity IV (2003) dataset.[5] Complete descriptions of these variables and those described below are available in Appendix 4.1.

Political Participation

For the regressions that look at media freedom and political participation, we rely on data from the World Values Survey 1999–2002, which questioned nearly 90 000 respondents, age 18 and over from 65 countries, about their level of political involvement. We eliminate countries for which there is no measure of media freedom, yielding a sample of more than 80 000 respondents from 61 countries.[6]

From this data we extract four measures of political participation which are willingness to: sign petitions, attend lawful demonstrations, participate in unofficial strikes, and occupy buildings in protest. We use these measures to construct four dependent variables for our regressions. We consider the impact of both measures of media freedom described above on each measure of political participation, only here we use scores for 2002 from Freedom House and Reporters Sans Frontières for each country where data are available. Data for our other variables, which include respondent age, income, education, and the frequency with which the respondent follows politics in the news, are also for 1999–2002 and come from the WVS. Finally, we again draw on Polity IV to measure democracy/autocracy in each country in 2000, and *World Development Indicators* (2004) for GNI per capita in each country in 2000.

Voter Turnout

To determine the relationship between media freedom and voter turnout we use data on voter turnout (measured as the number of votes divided by the population of voting age) in the most recent parliamentary election for which figures were available when these data were collected in 2005. We look at the same countries surveyed by the WVS on political participation and drop observations for which there are no data regarding media freedom, yielding a sample of 59 countries.[7]

Our measures of media freedom are from the same sources as above and we use scores for 2002. Data for additional variables, which include GNI per capita, average years of education, and democracy/autocracy for 2000 are from *World Development Indicators* (2004), the Barro-Lee (2000) dataset, *International Data on Educational Attainment: Updates and Implications*, and Polity IV respectively. Finally, data for whether or not a country has an active compulsory voting law come from the International Institute for Democracy and Electoral Assistance.

BENCHMARK RESULTS: MEDIA FREEDOM AND POLITICAL KNOWLEDGE

Figure 4.1 depicts the raw relationship between media freedom and political knowledge using the average political quiz score of citizens in each of the EU candidate countries and Freedom House's media freedom measure. The relationship is strong and positive. A freer media is associated with politically more knowledgeable citizens.

To econometrically isolate this connection we estimate the following equation using ordinary least-squares (OLS) with robust standard errors clustered by country:

$$\text{Quiz score}_{ic} = \beta_0 + \beta_1 \text{Media freedom}_c + \beta_2 \text{Income}_{ic}$$
$$+ \beta_3 \text{GNI per capita}_c + \beta_4 \text{Age}_{ic} + \beta_5 \text{Education}_{ic} + \beta_6 \text{Polity}_c$$
$$+ \beta_7 \text{Public expenditure on education}_c + \varepsilon_{ic} \qquad (4.1)$$

where Quiz score$_{ic}$ measures the basic political knowledge of citizen i in country c using her score on nine "true or false" questions about

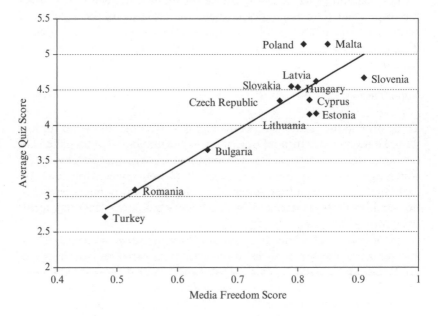

Source: Freedom House (2004) and Eurobarometer (ICPSR 2004)

Figure 4.1   Media freedom and political knowledge

simple political facts relating to the EU (her 'EU quiz score'). β_1, which measures the relationship between media freedom and political knowledge, is our parameter or interest, and ε_{ic} is a random error term. Media freedom$_c$ measures media freedom in country c using Freedom House's press freedom index. We want to control for exogenous individual characteristics that might affect quiz scores so we include Income$_{ic}$, which measures respondent income, Age$_{ic}$, which measures respondent age, and Education$_{ic}$, which measures respondent education level. To control for any impact of a country's average income on individual quiz scores, we include GNI per capita$_c$. We also want to account for institutional factors that may contribute to how an individual performs on the political quiz, such as how democratic or authoritarian the government is in her country and the quantity of resources her government devotes to education for its citizens. Polity$_c$ and Public expenditure on education$_c$ measure these items. Table 4.1 presents the results of this analysis.

We find a large, positive, and highly significant association between media freedom and political knowledge. Where the media is less free, citizens are less politically knowledgeable. In the default specifications in column 1, for example, falling from the highest level of media freedom

Table 4.1   Media freedom and political knowledge

	1	2
Media freedom	5.35[a]	4.86[a]
	(0.45)	(0.65)
Income		0.15[a]
		(0.01)
GNI per capita		−0.01
		(0.37)
Age		−0.08[b]
		(0.03)
Education		0.05[a]
		(0.01)
Polity		0.09
		(0.06)
Public expenditure on education		−0.01
		(0.12)
R^2	0.09	0.17
Observations	12 006	8 323

Notes: Regressand: quiz score. OLS (intercepts not reported) with robust standard errors clustered by country in parentheses. For detailed variable descriptions see Appendix 4.1. a=significant at 1%; b=significant at 5%.

in the sample to the lowest is associated with a 42 per cent increase in political ignorance. Stated differently, moving from the freest media in the sample to the least free is associated with a 0.96 standard deviation fall in political knowledge.

This relationship is similar when controls are included in column 2. After controlling for respondent income, age, and education, how democratic or authoritarian her government is, average income in her country, and how much is spent on public education in her country, falling from the country with the freest media in the sample to the country with the least free media is associated with a 37 per cent increase in political ignorance. This represents a 0.83 standard deviation decline in political knowledge. To put this in a slightly different perspective, going from the highest level of media freedom in the sample to the lowest means dropping from a quiz score average of (4.56/9 ≈) 51 per cent correct to a quiz score average of (2.86/9 ≈) 32 per cent correct.

Although all countries in our sample were EU candidates at the time the political quiz was administered, only one of them, Turkey, is not yet a full member. It is possible that citizens in Turkey expected the low likelihood of their nation becoming an EU member when the quiz was administered in 2003, and so were rationally more ignorant of basic EU political facts. In Figure 4.1, for example, Turkey has both the lowest quiz score and lowest media freedom. But perhaps Turkey's low quiz score is attributable to the relative unimportance of information about the EU for its citizens given the perceived unlikelihood of gaining membership, rather than to media freedom. To check if this is the case, we run the same regression in column 2, this time excluding Turkey from the sample. It is not. We find similar results to those we find when Turkey is not excluded. Media freedom's relationship to political knowledge remains large, positive, and highly significant.

MEDIA FREEDOM AND POLITICAL PARTICIPATION

A sizeable literature in political science empirically confirms that political knowledge and participation are mutually reinforcing (Klingemann 1979; Chong, McClosky and Zaller 1983; Luskin 1990; Junn 1991; Leighley 1991; Zaller 1992; Flanigan and Zingale 1994). The reason for this is straightforward. Where political knowledge is low, for instance because of low media freedom, the value of political participation is also low. With inadequate political knowledge, citizens find it more difficult to effectively monitor and punish self-serving politicians. In such an environment

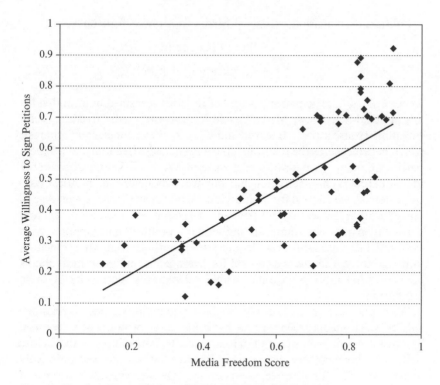

Source: Freedom House (2003) and WVS (1999–2002) (ICPSR 2005)

Figure 4.2 Media freedom and political participation

political participation is all cost and no benefit. The result is low political activeness. If low media freedom is associated with political ignorance, it should therefore also be associated with political apathy.

To determine this, we look at four measures of political participation: an individual's stated willingness to sign petitions, attend lawful demonstrations, join unofficial strikes, and occupy buildings in protest, or a stated history of having done these things. Figure 4.2 depicts the raw relationship between media freedom and political participation using individuals' willingness to sign petitions and Freedom House's media freedom measure. The relationship is clearly positive. A freer media is associated with a substantially greater willingness to sign petitions. To isolate the relationship between media freedom and political participation along this and other participatory dimensions, we estimate the following equation with OLS calculating standard errors robust to clustering by country:

$$\text{Political participation}_{ic} = \beta_0 + \beta_1 \text{Media freedom}_c + \beta_2 \text{Income}_{ic}$$
$$+ \beta_3 \text{GNI per capita}_c + \beta_4 \text{Age}_{ic}$$
$$+ \beta_5 \text{Education}_{ic} + \beta_6 \text{Polity}_c + \varepsilon_{ic} \qquad (4.2)$$

where Political participation$_{ic}$ is one of the four measures of an individual's political activeness; Media freedom$_c$ measures media freedom using Freedom House's press freedom index; β_1 is our coefficient of interest, which here measures the relationship between media freedom and political participation; and ε_{ic} is a random error term. We again want to account for individual-level characteristics that might partly determine political participation, so we control for an individual's income (Income$_{ic}$), age (Age$_{ic}$), and education (Education$_{ic}$). Likewise, we account for institutional factors that may partly determine an individual's political participation with Polity$_c$, which measures how democratic or authoritarian government is in her country. Finally, we control for average income in an individual's country using GNI per capita$_c$. Table 4.2 presents the results of these estimations.

We find a consistently sizeable, positive, and highly significant relationship between media freedom and these measures of political activeness. Our results retain their sign and significance after controlling for the factors discussed above. Where the media is less free, citizens are less politically active. Consider, for example, the relationship between media freedom and a citizen's willingness to sign petitions. After controlling for individual-level characteristics and country-level factors that might affect this willingness, moving from the country with the freest media in the sample to the one with the least media freedom is associated with a 54 per cent fall in citizens' willingness to sign petitions using the Freedom House measure. In other words, going from the freest media in the sample to the least free is associated with a 0.61 standard deviation drop in political activeness along this dimension. The other measures of political participation yield similar decreases in participation with decreases in media freedom.

MEDIA FREEDOM AND VOTER TURNOUT

Since voting is just another (though arguably more important) component of political activeness, if lower freedom in media is associated with reduced political knowledge, we should also observe lower voter turnout where the media is less free. Figure 4.3 depicts the raw relationship between media freedom and voter turnout using Freedom House's media freedom measure. According to the raw data, a freer media is associated with higher

Table 4.2 Media freedom and political participation

	Media freedom	Income	GNI per capita	Age	Education	Polity	R^2	N
Sign petitions	0.68[a] (0.09)						0.13	81 564
	0.31[b] (0.13)	0.01[a] (0.003)	0.11[a] (0.02)	−0.002 (0.007)	0.03[a] (0.004)	0.001 (0.004)	0.24	66 812
Attend lawful demonstrations	0.37[a] (0.07)						0.05	81 679
	0.20[c] (0.11)	0.005 (0.003)	0.03 (0.02)	−0.009 (0.007)	0.03[a] (0.003)	0.004 (0.004)	0.10	66 948
Join unofficial strikes	0.21[a] (0.03)						0.03	78 737
	0.12[b] (0.05)	0.002 (0.002)	0.02 (0.01)	−0.03[a] (0.004)	0.01[a] (0.002)	0.002 (0.002)	0.06	64 516
Occupy buildings	0.12[a] (0.03)						0.03	48 526
	0.08 (0.05)	0.002 (0.002)	0.02 (0.01)	−0.03[a] (0.006)	0.005[b] (0.002)	0.001 (0.002)	0.03	63 313

Notes: Regressand: sign petitions, attend lawful demonstrations, join unofficial strikes and occupy buildings. OLS (intercepts not reported) with robust standard errors clustered by country in parentheses. For detailed variable descriptions see Appendix 4.1. a = significant at 1%; b = significant at 5%; c = significant at 10%.

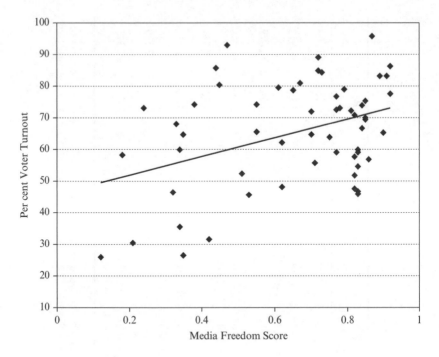

Source: Freedom House (2003) and IDEA (2005)

Figure 4.3   Media freedom and voter turnout

voter turnout. To isolate this relationship econometrically we estimate the following equation using OLS with robust standard errors:

$$\text{Voter turnout}_c = \beta_0 + \beta_1 \text{Media freedom}_c + \beta_2 \text{Compulsory voting}_c$$
$$+ \beta_3 \text{GNI per capita}_c + \beta_4 \text{Education}_c + \varepsilon_c \qquad (4.3)$$

where Voter turnout$_c$ is the number of votes cast in the most recent parliamentary election for which data were available, divided by the number of citizens of voting age in the country; β_1 is our coefficient of interest, which measures the relationship between media freedom and voter turnout; and ε_c is a random error term. Media freedom$_c$ measures a country's media freedom using the Freedom House index. Here it is important to control for the presence of active compulsory voting legislation in a country, which clearly impacts the level of voter turnout. We do this with Compulsory voting$_c$, a binary variable that is equal to unity if a country has such a law and zero otherwise. We also include controls for a country's per capita income (GNI per capita$_c$) and the average years of education an

Table 4.3   Media freedom and voter turnout

	1	2
Media freedom	26.51[b]	49.41[a]
	(11.00)	(15.44)
Compulsory voting		5.90
		(5.08)
GNI per capita		−1.00
		(2.23)
Education		−1.56
		(1.23)
R^2	0.10	0.26
Observations	59	52

Notes: Regressand: voter turnout. OLS (intercepts not reported) with robust standard errors in parentheses. For detailed variable descriptions see Appendix 4.1. a=significant at 1%; b=significant at 5%.

individual receives in their country (Education$_c$). Table 4.3 presents the results of these regressions.

The relationship between media freedom and voter turnout is consistent with our findings for the relationship between media freedom and political knowledge and participation. It is large, positive, and highly significant, even after controlling for income, age, education, and compulsory voting laws. Where the media is less free, citizens vote less. After accounting for these other factors, moving from the country with the freest media in the sample to the one with the least media freedom is associated with falling from approximately 77 per cent voter turnout to approximately 38 per cent voter turnout. Stated differently, going from the country with most free media in the sample to the least free is associated with a 2.41 standard deviation reduction in voter turnout.[8]

SENSITIVITY ANALYSES

We take a number of measures to ensure the robustness of these findings. First, we re-estimate the fully specified equation (column 2) in Table 4.1 that looks at the relationship between media freedom and political knowledge, this time adding additional controls for 1) whether or not the respondent has ever heard of the EU or 2) has ever heard of the European Parliament, 3) how much television, radio and daily paper news they consume, and 4) how much attention they say they pay to EU-related news. These items may be endogenous to a citizen's score on the EU quiz, so we have excluded them from the main regressions. We include them here only as a test of robustness. The results of these re-estimations are presented in Table 4.4. Although for both measures of media freedom the coefficient of interest drops, both remain large, positive, and highly significant.

Table 4.4   Sensitivity analysis for political knowledge

	1	2
Media freedom (FH)	4.39[a]	
	(0.61)	
Media freedom (RSF)		3.39[b]
		(0.57)
TV news consumption	0.26[c]	0.30[c]
	(0.14)	(0.14)
Daily paper news consumption	0.51[a]	0.53[a]
	(0.11)	(0.12)
Radio news consumption	0.16[a]	0.17[a]
	(0.04)	(0.05)
Attention to EU news	0.58[a]	0.57[a]
	(0.05)	(0.04)
Heard of EU	0.62[b]	0.71[b]
	(0.23)	(0.23)
Heard of European Parliament	1.30[a]	1.32[a]
	(0.09)	(0.09)
Income	0.08[a]	0.08[a]
	(0.01)	(0.01)
GNI per capita	−0.24	−0.19
	(0.34)	(0.43)
Age	−0.11[a]	−0.13[a]
	(0.03)	(0.03)
Education	0.03[a]	0.03[a]
	(0.01)	(0.01)
Polity	0.12[b]	0.10
	(0.05)	(0.06)
Public expenditure on education	−0.02	0.30[b]
	(0.11)	(0.13)
R^2	0.29	0.29
Observations	8 014	8 014

Notes: Regressand: quiz score. OLS (intercepts not reported) with robust standard errors clustered by country in parentheses. For detailed variable descriptions see Appendix 4.1. a=significant at 1%; b=significant at 5%; c=significant at 10%.

Table 4.5 With 'Heard of EU' and 'Heard of EU Parliament' as dependent variable

	Heard of EU		Heard of European Parliament	
Media freedom (FH)	0.04[b]		0.46[a]	
	(0.02)		(0.09)	
Media freedom (RSF)		−0.003		0.20[a]
		(0.02)		(0.07)
Income	0.002[b]	0.001[b]	0.02[a]	0.02[a]
	(0.001)	(0.001)	(0.002)	(0.003)
GNI per capita	0.007	−0.001	0.11[b]	0.10
	(0.006)	(0.008)	(0.05)	(0.06)
Age	−0.002[b]	−0.002[b]	−0.01[b]	−0.01[b]
	(0.001)	(0.001)	(0.01)	(0.01)
Education	0.001[b]	0.001[a]	0.01[a]	0.01[b]
	(0.000)	(0.000)	(0.001)	(0.006)
Polity	0.001	0.002	−0.004	−0.004
	(0.001)	(0.001)	(0.007)	(0.007)
Public expenditure on education	−0.003[c]	0.003	−0.04[a]	−0.001
	(0.001)	(0.003)	(0.01)	(0.01)
Observations	8 380	8 380	8 239	8 239
R^2	0.01	0.01	0.06	0.05

Notes: Regressand: Heard of EU and Heard of EU Parliament. OLS with robust standard errors clustered by country in parentheses. For detailed variable descriptions see Appendix 4.1. a=significant at 1%; b=significant at 5%; c=significant at 10%.

Second, we try using whether or not an individual has ever heard of the EU and whether she has ever heard of the European Parliament as dependent variables. If a citizen in an EU candidate country has never heard of the EU or the European Parliament, it is probably safe to say that her political knowledge is quite low. These variables therefore provide alternative measures of political knowledge. We consider the relationship between media freedom and these measures of political knowledge in Table 4.5. The results are the same as when we use citizens' EU quiz scores to measure political knowledge. Media freedom is, in all cases but one, positive and significant. Where the media is less free, citizens of candidate countries to the EU are less likely to have heard of the EU or the European Parliament.

As another check, we examine the relationship between media freedom and the amount of media-provided news individuals consume. It stands to reason that where media-provided information is poor,

Media, development, and institutional change

Table 4.6   The impact of media freedom on media-provided news consumption

	TV news consumption		Daily paper news consumption		Radio news consumption	
Media freedom (FH)	−0.08 (0.09)		0.65^b (0.25)		0.98^a (0.14)	
Media freedom (RSF)		−0.24^a (0.04)		0.43^c (0.23)		0.83^a (0.08)
Income	0.01^b (0.003)	0.009^b (0.003)	0.03^a (0.004)	0.03^a (0.004)	0.007^a (0.002)	0.008^a (0.002)
GNI per capita	−0.13^a (0.03)	−0.16^a (0.02)	0.05 (0.10)	0.04 (0.09)	−0.06 (0.06)	−0.04 (0.06)
Age	0.05^a (0.01)	0.05^a (0.01)	0.02^a (0.01)	0.02^a (0.01)	0.05^a (0.01)	0.04^a (0.01)
Education	0.002^b (0.001)	0.003^b (0.001)	0.007^a (0.001)	0.007^a (0.001)	0.003^c (0.001)	0.002 (0.001)
Polity	−0.004 (0.005)	0.001 (0.003)	−0.02^c (0.01)	−0.02^c (0.01)	−0.01^c (0.01)	−0.02^b (0.01)
Public expenditure on education	0.04^a (0.01)	0.05^a (0.01)	−0.02 (0.04)	0.03 (0.03)	−0.001 (0.02)	0.07^a (0.01)
Observations	8 409	8 409	8 405	8 405	8 406	8 406
R^2	0.06	0.06	0.11	0.10	0.11	0.11

Notes: Regressand: TV news consumption, radio news consumption, and daily paper news consumption. OLS with robust standard errors clustered by country in parentheses. For detailed variable descriptions see Appendix 4.1. a=significant at 1%; b=significant at 5%; c=significant at 10%.

citizens will consume less of it. Thus, if low media freedom generates poorly informed citizens, we should expect citizens in those countries to consume less media-provided news than citizens in nations where the media is freer. We check to see if this is the case in Table 4.6. In several instances it is.

We break down media news consumption by the type of media involved: television, radio, and daily papers. Lower media freedom is associated with significantly lower radio and paper-provided news consumption using both the Freedom House and Reporters Sans Frontières measures. TV news consumption is the exception here. This is negatively related to media freedom (though, in only one case significantly). Where media freedom is lower, it appears, citizens consume more television-provided news.

Table 4.7   Sensitivity analysis for political participation

	Media freedom (FH)	Media freedom (RSF)
Sign petitions	0.33[b]	0.41[a]
	(0.14)	(0.11)
Attend lawful demonstrations	0.19[c]	0.26[b]
	(0.10)	(0.10)
Join unofficial strikes	0.12[b]	0.15[a]
	(0.06)	(0.06)
Occupy buildings	0.09[c]	0.14[c]
	(0.05)	(0.07)

Notes: Regressand: in left column. OLS (intercepts not reported) with robust standard errors clustered by country. Variables included but not reported: follow politics in the news, income, GNI per capita, age, education, and polity. For detailed variable descriptions see Appendix 4.1. a=significant at 1%; b=significant at 5%; c=significant at 10%.

Third, we perform a similar sensitivity analysis for the regressions relating to political participation. In addition to the controls already used, we add a variable that measures the extent to which an individual reports that she follows politics in the news. As above, we exclude this variable from the main regressions because of the potential for endogeneity. It is included here only as a test of robustness. The results of this estimation are in Table 4.7 and are virtually identical. Media freedom remains sizeable, positive, and significant for all four measures of political participation and across both measures of media freedom.

Fourth, we check to see if our results for political participation and voter turnout are driven by a particular region. In Table 4.8 we include five regional dummies and find similar results. Media freedom's relationship to political participation and voter turnout is similar to the results presented earlier; however, using the Reporters Sans Frontières measure, it becomes insignificant in several cases.

Fifth, we re-run all of the regressions in Tables 4.1, 4.2 and 4.3, which look at the relationship between media freedom and political knowledge, political participation, and voter turnout respectively, using an alternative measure of media freedom to the Freedom House measure to see if this changes the results. Our new measures are the Reporters Sans Frontières measure described earlier in this chapter and the measure created by Shleifer and Treisman (2005), who look at the number of cases of state censorship, "legal suppression," and imprisonment of journalists from the International Press Institute, and weight this figure by the number of daily newspapers in each country with data from UNESCO,

Table 4.8   With regional dummies

	Media freedom (FH)	Media freedom (RSF)
Sign petitions	0.23^c	0.19
	(0.12)	(0.15)
Attend lawful demonstrations	0.12	0.06
	(0.13)	(0.16)
Join unofficial strikes	0.12^b	0.20^b
	(0.06)	(0.09)
Occupy buildings	0.05	0.16
	(0.06)	(0.11)
Voter turnout	44.05^a	53.48^c
	(16.22)	(30.14)

Notes: Regressand: in left column. OLS (intercepts not reported) with robust standard errors clustered by country. Variables included but not reported: for sign petitions, attend lawful demonstrations, join unofficial strikes, and occupy buildings: income, GNI per capita, age, education, polity, European continent dummy, African continent dummy, North American continent dummy, South American continent dummy, and Asian dummy. For voter turnout: GNI per capita, education, compulsory voting, European continent dummy, African continent dummy, North American continent dummy, South American continent dummy, and Asian dummy. All dummies are equal to one if a country is in that region and zero otherwise. For detailed variable descriptions see Appendix 4.1. a=significant at 1%; b=significant at 5%; c=significant at 10%.

to provide a measure of journalist suppression in each country for the period 1999–2000. Like the Freedom House measure, the Reporters Sans Frontières measure is a measure of media freedom. We should therefore be looking for a positive sign on the coefficient of interest in these regressions for the results to be consistent with our findings using the Freedom House measure reported in our benchmark tables above. In contrast, the "legal suppression" measure is a measure of how unfree the media is in a nation. We should therefore be looking for a negative sign on the coefficient of interest in these regressions for these results to be consistent with our findings using the other two measures of media freedom. Table 4.9 presents these results.

Using the Reporters Sans Frontières measure of media freedom, we find similar results to those produced using the Freedom House measure, supporting the findings in the tables above. Using the journalist suppression measure, we also find consistent results. The relationship between journalist suppression and political knowledge is sizeable, negative, and significant, even after controlling for other factors. The results are also negative and significant for willingness to attend lawful demonstrations. Journalist

Table 4.9   Using journalist suppression

	RSF measure of media freedom	Journalist suppression
Quiz score	3.52[a]	−0.73[a]
	(0.71)	(0.10)
Sign petitions	0.31[b]	0.01
	(0.12)	(0.02)
Attend lawful demonstrations	0.19	−0.04[a]
	(0.12)	(0.01)
Join unofficial strikes	0.14[b]	−0.01
	(0.06)	(0.01)
Occupy buildings	0.19[b]	−0.001
	(0.09)	(0.001)
Voter turnout	48.82[c]	−1.40
	(24.95)	(4.23)

Notes: Regressand: in left column. OLS (intercepts not reported) with robust standard errors clustered by country. Variables included but not reported: for quiz score: income, GNI per capita, age, and education. For sign petitions, attend lawful demonstrations, join unofficial strikes, and occupy buildings: income, GNI per capita, age, education, and polity. For voter turnout: GNI per capita, years of education, and compulsory voting. For detailed variable descriptions see Appendix 4.1. a=significant at 1%; b=significant at 5%; c=significant at 10%.

suppression's association with the remaining political activeness measures and voter turnout is insignificant, though nearly always negative.

SUMMATION

Our exploration of the 'black box' surrounding the channel that links media, information, and development leads to several conclusions. First, low media freedom is strongly associated with poor political knowledge, low political participation, and low voter turnout. The reverse is true for countries with higher media freedom. All three of these results are robust to sample, specification, and alternative measures of media freedom. While they cannot be decisively interpreted as causal, these results do suggest that low media freedom is an important factor contributing to political ignorance and apathy. The correspondence between the "triangulated" evidence should strengthen our confidence in this relationship.

The connections established by these findings illuminate the link between media ownership and development identified by Djankov *et al.*

(2003) on the one hand, and the importance of the media in informing the electorate identified by Besley and Burgess (2002) among others, on the other hand. In light of their studies, our analysis finds evidence that supports the following specific channel of connection: where the state controls the media, citizens are politically more ignorant and apathetic. More politically ignorant and apathetic citizens find it harder to effectively monitor or punish the activities of self-interested politicians. Less checked by voters, politicians find it easier to pursue privately beneficial policies at the expense of society. As a result, the Reformers' Dilemma is more likely to persist, making the adoption of reforms conducive to development more difficult. In contrast, where the media is free, citizens are more politically knowledgeable and active, facilitating their ability to reward politicians who pursue social welfare-enhancing reforms and punish politicians who cater to special interests, overcoming the Reformers' Dilemma.

Our findings also have potential implications for the role of media and institutional change. Recall that where the state owns the media, political leaders will tend to use the media to reinforce existing policies and institutions by limiting criticism and exposure to alternative information. In using media in this way, these leaders run the risk of generating an unintended "preference gap" where private preferences for change diverge from the status quo. We should expect this gap to be relatively large in societies where the media is unfree because citizens are unable to reveal their true preferences. Where such a gap exists, punctuated institutional change is more likely. In contrast, where media is free, one would expect a diverse media representing a wide variety of views and ideas. As such, we would expect the preference gap between true private preferences and publicly revealed preferences to be small and the likelihood of punctuated change to be less relative to societies with an unfree media.

ACKNOWLEDGEMENTS

This chapter is based on Leeson (2008). Revisions have been made to the introduction and conclusion for purposes of consistency with our overall analysis but the core argument and analysis of the chapter remains the same.

NOTES

1. Van Belle *et al.* (2004) examine the ability of an independent media to compel non-elected policy officials to serve the public's interest. Dyck and Zingales (2002) consider

how a free media improves the accuracy of media-provided information in the context of corporate governance.

2. For a review of this expansive literature see for instance Verba and Nie (1972), Wolfinger and Rosenstone (1980), Dalton and Wattenberg (1993), Rosenstone and Hansen (1993), Verba *et al.* (1995), Niemi and Weisberg (2001), Dalton (2002). Gentzkow (2005) provides an especially interesting examination of television consumption's impact on voter turnout. See also Althaus and Trautman (2005), who investigate the impact of television market size on voter turnout. Ahrend (2002) and Brunetti and Weder (2003) consider the relationship between press freedom and corruption. Both find that higher press freedom is associated with lower corruption.

3. The complete list of T or F questions is as follows (correct answer in parentheses): 1) The EU is made of 15 states (T); 2) The European Community was created after WWI (F); 3) The European flag is bright blue with yellow stars (T); 4) There are 15 stars on the European flag (F); 5) Headquarters of the EU are in Brussels, Strasbourg and Luxembourg (T); 6) Members of the European Parliament are directly elected by the citizens of the EU (T); 7) There is a President of the EU directly elected by all the citizens (F); 8) The EU has its own anthem (T); 9) There are no borders between the EU (T).

4. Malta was not included in the Polity IV dataset and does not have a media freedom score from Reporters Sans Frontières. In the regressions that consider political knowledge, Malta is therefore included only in the benchmark specification using Freedom House's data.

5. For all regression, when Polity scores for 2000 were unavailable, the closest available scores were employed.

6. These countries are: Albania, Algeria, Argentina, Austria, Bangladesh, Belarus, Belgium, Bosnia, Bulgaria, Canada, Chile, Croatia, Czech Republic, Denmark, Egypt, Estonia, Finland, France, Germany, Greece, Hungary, Iceland, India, Indonesia, Ireland, Israel, Italy, Japan, Jordan, Korea, Latvia, Lithuania, Luxembourg, Malta, Mexico, Montenegro, Netherlands, Nigeria, Pakistan, Peru, Philippines, Poland, Portugal, Romania, Russia, Serbia, Singapore, Slovakia, Slovenia, South Africa, Spain, Sweden, Tanzania, Turkey, Uganda, Ukraine, United Kingdom, United States, Venezuela, Vietnam, and Zimbabwe. The WVS was administered to approximately 1000 respondents in each country with the exception of South Africa, Egypt and Turkey, which surveyed 3000, 3000 and 3401 respondents respectively.

7. These countries are the same as those listed above with the following deletions: Montenegro, Serbia, and Vietnam, and the following addition: Iran.

8. We also estimate the relationship between media freedom and voter turnout, excluding countries with compulsory voting laws. The results are similar.

REFERENCES

Ahrend, Rudiger (2002) "Press Freedom, Human Capital and Corruption," mimeo.

Althaus, Scott and Todd Trautman (2005) "The Impact of Television Market Size on Voter Turnout in American Elections," University of Illinois at Urbana-Champaign, mimeo.

Barro, Robert and Jong-Wha Lee (2000) *International Data on Educational Attainment: Updates and Implications*, CID Working Paper No. 42, www.cid. harvard.edu/cidwp/pdf/042.pdf, accessed 11 January 2009.

Besley, Timothy and Robin Burgess (2002) "The Political Economy of Government Responsiveness: Theory and Evidence from India," *Quarterly Journal of Economics*, 117: 1415–1452.

Besley, Timothy and Andrea Prat (2006) "Handcuffs for the Grabbing Hand? Media Capture and Government Accountability," *American Economic Review*, 96: 720–736.

Brunetti, Aymo and Beatrice Weder (2003) "A Free Press is Bad News for Corruption," *Journal of Public Economics*, 87: 1801–1824.

Chong, Dennis, Herbert McClosky and John Zaller (1983) "Patterns of Support for Democratic and Capitalist Values," *British Journal of Political Science*, 13: 401–440.

Coyne, Christopher and Peter Leeson (2004) "Read All About It! Understanding the Role of Media in Economic Development," *Kyklos*, 57: 21–44.

Dalton, Russell (2002) *Citizen Politics*. 3rd ed. New York: Chatham House.

Dalton, Russell and Martin Wattenberg (1993) "The Not So Simple Act of Voting." In A.W. Finifter (ed.), *Political Science: The State of the Discipline II*. Washington DC: American Political Science Association, pp. 193–218.

Djankov, Simeon, Caralee McLiesh, Tatiana Nenova, and Andrei Shleifer (2003) "Who Owns the Media?" *Journal of Law and Economics*, 46: 341–382.

Dyck, Alexander and Luigi Zingales (2002) 'The Corporate Governance Role of the Media'. In Alisa Clapp-Itnyre, Roumeen Islam and Caralee McLiesh (eds), *The Right to Tell: The Role of Mass Media in Economic Development*. Washington DC: The World Bank, pp. 107–140.

Flanigan, William H. and Nancy H. Zingale (1994) *Political Behavior in the American Electorate*. Washington, DC: CQ Press.

Freedom House (2003) *Freedom of the Press 2003: A Global Survey of Media Independence*. New York: Rowman and Littlefield.

Freedom of the Press (2004) *Freedom of the press 2004: A Global Survey of Media Independence*. New York: Rowman and Littlefield.

Gentzkow, Matthew (2005) "Television and Voter Turnout," University of Chicago, mimeo.

ICPSR (2005) *European and World Values Surveys Integrated Data File 1999–2002, Release I*, Study No. 3975, www.icpsr.org/cgi-bin/summholdings?study=3975&path=ICPSR, accessed 11 January 2009.

ICPSR (2004) Candidate Countries Eurobarometer 2003.4, Study No. 4056, www.icpsr.org/cgi-bin/summholdings?study=4056&path=ICPSR, accessed 11 January 2009.

Junn, Jane (1991) "Participation and Political Knowledge." In William Crotty (ed.), *Political Participation and American Democracy*. New York: Greenwood Press, pp. 193–212.

Klingemann, Hans (1979). "Ideological Conceptualization and Political Action." In Samuel Barnes and Max Kaase (eds), *Political Action: Mass Participation in Five Western Democracies*. Beverly Hills, CA: Sage, pp. 279–304.

Leeson, Peter T. (2008) "Media Freedom, Political Knowledge, and Participation," *Journal of Economic Perspectives*, 22(2): 155–169.

Leighley, Jan (1991) "Participation as a Stimulus of Political Conceptualization," *Journal of Politics*, 53: 198–211.

Luskin, Robert (1990) "Explaining Political Sophistication," *Political Behavior*, 12: 331–361.

Niemi, Richard and Herbert Weisberg (2001) "Why is Voter Turnout Low (and Why is it Declining)?" In Richard Niemi and Herbert Weisberg (eds), *Controversies in Voting Behavior*. Washington, DC: CQ Press, pp. 22–37.

Polity IV Project (2003) *Polity IV Dataset: Political Regime Characteristics and*

Transitions, 1800–2003. Center for International Development and Conflict Management, University of Maryland, College Park, Maryland, www.systemic-peace.org/polity/polity4.htm, accessed 11 January 2009.

Prat, Andrea and David Stromberg (2005) *Commercial Television and Voter Information,* CEPR Discussion Paper no. 4989, www.cepr.org/pubs/new-dps/dplist.asp?dpno=4989, accessed 11 January 2009.

Reporters Sans Frontières (2002) *First World Press Freedom Ranking,* http://www.rsf.org/article.php3?id_article=4116.

Reporters Sans Frontières (2003) *Second World War Freedom Rankings,* http://www.rsf.org/article.php3?id_article=8247.

Rosenstone, Steven and John Hansen (1993) *Mobilization, Participation, and Democracy in America.* New York: Macmillan.

Sen, Amartya (1984) *Poverty and Famines.* Oxford: Oxford University Press.

Sen, Amartya (1999) *Development as Freedom.* New York: Alfred A. Knopf Inc.

Shleifer, Andrei and Daniel Treisman (2005) "A Normal Country: Russia After Communism," *Journal of Economic Perspectives,* 19: 151–174.

Snyder, James and David Stromberg (2004) "Media Markets' Impact on Politics," mimeo.

Stromberg, David (2004) "Radio's Impact on Public Spending," *Quarterly Journal of Economics,* 119: 189–221.

Van Belle, Douglas, Jean-Sebastien Rioux and David Potter (2004) *Media, Bureaucracies, and Foreign Aid: A Comparative Analysis of the United States, United Kingdom, Canada, France and Japan.* New York: Palgrave/St. Martin.

Verba, Sidney and Norman Nie (1972) *Participation in America: Political Democracy and Social Equality.* Chicago, IL: University of Chicago Press.

Verba, Sidney, Kay Lehman Schlozman, and Henry Brady (1995) *Voice and Equality: Civic Voluntarism in American Politics.* Cambridge, MA: Harvard University Press.

Wolfinger, Raymond and Steven Rosenstone (1980) *Who Votes?* New Haven, CT: Yale University Press.

World Bank (2004) *World Development Indicators,* CD ROM.

Zaller, John (1992) *The Nature and Origins of Mass Opinion.* Cambridge: Cambridge University Press.

APPENDIX 4.1

Table 4A.1   Descriptions of variables

Variable	Description
Age	
For political knowledge:	Age group of respondent scaled from 1–4 where 1 = 15–24 years, 2 = 25–39 years, 3 = 40–54 years, 4 = 55+ years, 2003. Source: Eurobarometer (ICPSR 2004).
For political participation:	Age group of respondent scaled from 1–3 where 1 = 15–29 years, 2 = 30–49 years, 3 = 50+ years, 1999–2002. Source: WVS (ICPSR 2005).
Attend lawful demonstrations	Index of respondent's willingness to attend lawful demonstrations, rescaled from 0–1 so that 0 = "would never do," 0.5 = "might do," and 1 = "have done," 1999–2002. Source: WVS (ICPSR 2005).
Attention to EU news	Self-reported degree to which respondent pays attention to news related to the EU. Scaled from 1–3 where 1 = "no attention at all," 2 = "a little attention" and 3 = "a lot of attention," 2003. Source: Eurobarometer (ICPSR 2004).
Polity	Index of democracy/autocracy, 2000 (or closest available year). A −10 to 10 scale constructed by subtracting the degree of political institution closedness (autocracy score) from the degree of political institution openness (democracy score). Higher scores indicate greater openness. Source: Polity IV Project (2003).
Compulsory voting	A binary variable that is equal to 1 if a country had and enforced a law compelling its citizens to vote in the most recent parliamentary election for which data were available and is equal to zero otherwise. Source: International Institute for Democracy and Electoral Assistance (2005).
Daily paper news consumption	Frequency with which respondent reads the news in daily papers, rescaled from 0–1 where 1 = "every day," 0.75 = "several times a week," 0.5 = "once or twice a week," and 0 = "less often," 2003. Source: Eurobarometer (ICPSR 2004).
Education	
For political knowledge:	Respondent's age when s/he stopped full-time education, 2003. Source: Eurobarometer (ICPSR 2004).
For political participation:	Scale of educational attainment from 1–8 where a higher score means a greater level of attainment, 1999–2002. Source: WVS (ICPSR 2005).
For voter turnout:	Average number of years of primary through post-secondary schooling for citizens aged 15 and over in 2000, except for

Table 4A.1 (continued)

Variable	Description
	Estonia, Latvia and Lithuania, which are for 1990. Source: Barro and Lee (2000).
Follow politics in the news	Frequency with which respondent follows politics on television, the radio or in daily papers, rescaled from 0–1 where 1 = "every day," 0.75 = "several times a week," 0.5 = "once or twice a week," and 0 = "less often," 1999–2002. Source: WVS (ICPSR 2005).
GNI per capita	Gross national income per capita in US$10,000, 2000. Source: World Bank (2004).
Heard of EU	A binary variable that is equal to 1 if a respondent has heard of the EU, 2003. Source: Eurobarometer (ICPSR 2004).
Heard of European Parliament	A binary variable that is equal to 1 if a respondent has heard of the European Parliament, 2003. Source: Eurobarometer (ICPSR 2004).
Income	
For political knowledge:	Self-reported income decile of respondent where 1 is the lowest income decile and 10 is the highest, 2003. Source: Eurobarometer (ICPSR 2004).
For political participation:	Same as above only for 1999–2002. Source: WVS (ICPSR 2005).
Join unofficial strikes	Index of respondent's willingness to join unofficial strikes rescaled from 0–1 so that 0 = "would never do," 0.5 = "might do," and 1 = "have done," 1999–2002. Source: WVS (ICPSR 2005).
Journalist suppression	Total number of cases of state censorship, "suppression by law" and imprisonment of journalists for the period 1999–2000 according to the International Press Institute, divided by the total number of daily newspapers as reported by UNESCO. Source: Shleifer and Treisman (2005).
Media freedom (FH)	
For political knowledge:	Freedom House index of media freedom, 2003. Each country is rated in three areas of potential state influence over the media: legal environment, political influences and economic pressures, to determine an overall score. Score rescaled from 0–1 where a higher score means more freedom. Source: Freedom House (2004).
For political participation and voter turnout:	Same as above only for 2002. Source: Freedom House (2003).

Table 4A.1   (continued)

Variable	Description
Media freedom (RSF)	
For political knowledge:	Reporters Sans Frontières index of media freedom, 2003. Scores are composed by asking journalists, researchers and legal experts to answer 50 questions relating to a range of press freedom violations, such as murders or arrests of journalists, censorship, pressure, state monopolies in various fields, punishment of press law offences and regulation of the media, to determine an overall score. Score rescaled from 0–1 where a higher score means more freedom. Source: Reporters Sans Frontières (2003).
For political participation and voter turnout:	Same as above only for 2002. Source: Reporters Sans Frontières (2002).
Occupy buildings	Index of respondent's willingness to occupy buildings or factories in protest rescaled from 0–1 so that 0 = "would never do," 0.5 = "might do," and 1 = "have done," 1999–2002. Source: WVS (ICPSR 2005).
Public expenditure on education	Government expenditure on education, including subsidies to private education at the primary, secondary and tertiary levels, as a percentage of GDP, 2003. Source: World Bank (2004).
Quiz score	Number of correctly answered True or False questions about basic EU-related political facts (out of nine), 2003. Quiz administered to citizens 15+ years old. Source: Eurobarometer (ICPSR 2004).
Radio news consumption	Frequency with which respondent listens to the news on the radio, rescaled from 0–1 where 1 = "every day," 0.75 = "several times a week," 0.5 = "once or twice a week," and 0 = "less often," 2003. Source: Eurobarometer (ICPSR 2004).
Sign petitions	Index of respondent's willingness to sign petitions rescaled from 0–1 so that 0 = "would never do," 0.5 = "might do," and 1 = "have done," 1999–2002. Source: WVS (ICPSR 2005).
TV news consumption	Frequency with which respondent watches the news on television, rescaled from 0–1 where 1 = "every day," 0.75 = "several times a week," 0.5 = "once or twice a week," and 0 = "less often," 2003. Source: Eurobarometer (ICPSR 2004).
Voter turnout	The total number of votes in the most recent parliamentary election for which data were available divided by the population of voting age. Source: International Institute for Democracy and Electoral Assistance (2005).

5. Case studies of media, institutions, and the Reformers' Dilemma

INTRODUCTION

The previous chapter provided a statistical analysis of the relationship between media freedom and citizens' political knowledge and political participation. These findings provide evidence that citizens are more politically ignorant and apathetic in those countries where government has greater control over the media. This analysis is important for quantifying the impact of state involvement in the media and for identifying the channel that links media, information, and development. However, these statistical tests do not directly capture the key causal mechanisms central to our overall argument. For example, the statistical analysis fails to capture the full array of ways government manipulates the media or the process through which an independent press emerges. Further, the previous analysis does not provide detailed insight into media's dual roles as a catalyst of change and a mechanism for reinforcing changes, or into media's three effects—gradual effect, punctuation effect, and reinforcement effect—on policy and institutional change.

We complement the previous chapter's statistical analysis with three country case studies—Mexico, Russia, and Poland. These allow us to explore the various causal mechanisms presented in previous chapters in more detail, while paying careful attention to the specific context in which the media exists and evolves. Because the trajectory of a country's media cannot be separated from its political, economic, and social contexts, this method is fitting for our topic of study. For each case we consider media's historical background, the factors that contributed to increases or decreases in media freedom, and media's impact on the institutions of the country under consideration. We pay particular attention to media's dual roles and to its three effects on policy and institutional change. We conclude each case with a brief discussion of the key lessons and insights for our overall analysis.

Our choice of countries came from the desire to analyze situations where the media had varying levels of success in generating policy and institutional change, as well as a solution to the Reformers' Dilemma. We first consider the case of media in Mexico and focus specifically on the process through which the media has emerged in facilitating a solution to the Reformers' Dilemma. Mexico provides an interesting case study for our theory of the role of media in policy and institutional change. It is considered a newly industrialized country and its political institutions are still evolving (see Bożyk 2006: 164). As we discuss below, the 2000 elections were an important event in Mexico because they signaled a break from the past. With the defeat of the corrupt Institutional Revolutionary Party, many viewed the elections as an important step toward genuine freedom and democracy in Mexico. As such, Mexico serves as a case where the media contributed to change for the better but where the final outcome of these changes is still uncertain.

The subsequent two cases focus on the role of media in two transition countries—Russia and Poland. The transition of formerly communist countries provides an interesting laboratory to study the role of media (Carrington and Nelson 2002: 232). We consider Poland and Russia for several reasons. Poland is the largest of the eight former communist countries to join the European Community. Further, it is generally considered a successful transition country (see, for example, Jackson, Klich and Poznanska 2005; Leeson and Trumbull 2006). Russia was at the center of the USSR and largest of the successor states. Relative to Poland it has not successfully transitioned to democracy or capitalism (Leeson and Trumbull 2006). Finally, and perhaps most importantly, both countries underwent significant but different institutional changes following communism's collapse, creating a useful "natural experiment" to explore media's effect on institutions. Russia is a case where media contributed to change, but that change was not institutionalized. In other words, media failed to provide a sustainable solution to the Reformers' Dilemma. In Poland, in contrast, the media not only served as a catalyst of change, but also served to reinforce beneficial reforms by providing a solution to the Reformers' Dilemma. In sum, Russia is a case where the media failed to solve the Reformers' Dilemma while Poland is a case where media was successful in this role. Mexico sits between these two cases because while media played an important role as a catalyst of change, the ultimate result remains uncertain.

The issues associated with attempts to reform economic and political institutions following communism's collapse fit well with our Reformers' Dilemma model. This allows us to analyze the factors that were effective, or ineffective, in solving the fundamental dilemma present in any reform effort. In each case we focus on media's role prior to communism's collapse to understand how it was embedded in these countries' larger economic, political, and social contexts. We then consider what happened to the media following communism's collapse in each nation. We focus in particular on the array of factors that contributed to or prevented the emergence of media as a solution to the Reformers' Dilemma.

During the communist period in Russia the media was a central part of the Soviet propaganda system. After communism's collapse the media failed to be separated from the political system for a variety of reasons we discuss in detail. The lack of a clean break between the media and political apparatus ultimately resulted in media's failure to solve the Reformers' Dilemma. Similar to Russia, the media was a key tool for control in communist Poland. However, in contrast to Russia, clear steps were taken to separate the media from the political system following the collapse of communism in Poland. This allowed for the emergence of a truly independent media, which played an important role in overcoming the Reformers' Dilemma. Considering these two cases in detail allows us to clearly isolate the factors that influenced media's success or failure as a solution to the Reformers' Dilemma.

MEXICO

Historical Background of the Mexican Media

Mexico was ruled by the Institutional Revolutionary Party (PRI) from the 1930s through the late 1990s. Although the PRI presented the image of a regime upholding liberal democratic values, in practice things were very different. Opposition parties were repressed and elections were fraudulent. In the absence of checks and balances, the PRI's hold on power was self-enforcing due to a complex system of corruption that benefited the PRI's members at the expense of Mexican citizens. Peruvian author Mario Vargas-Llosa (1991) dubbed Mexico's political system "the perfect dictatorship" because of the stability of the PRI's grasp on power. In terms of the Reformers' Dilemma framework developed in Chapter 2, the situation in Mexico under the PRI was characterized by the "defection" equilibrium whereby political officials catered to special interests at the expense of the broader Mexican populace. Further, as we will discuss, those in power used the media to reinforce the status quo.

However, several major events weakened the PRI's established position over two decades. The first event was the economic downturn in the early 1980s. Leading up to this period, most Mexican industries were nationalized and relied heavily on government subsidies. The magnitude and extent of these subsidies placed the government under increasing financial pressure, especially during the economic downturn. Further, corruption dominated the political system and the weight of this corruption stifled the economy's productive aspects. In short the state apparatus became so large and expensive that the Mexican economy could no longer afford to support it (see Lawson 2002: 16–18). This led to national bankruptcy in 1982, which in turn led to calls for significant economic reforms.

The result was a series of economic reforms under President Carlos Salinas (1988–1994) aimed at allowing the PRI to maintain its position of power in the wake of the public's calls for change. The reforms included anti-inflationary programs, cuts in government spending, the privatization of state assets, changes to the tax code, reduced trade barriers and regulations, and reduced barriers to foreign direct investment in Mexico. Salinas and the PRI undertook many of these reforms reluctantly. While they realized that the reforms would reduce their absolute power, they also realized that ceding some power was preferable to the possibility of losing complete control over the country due to economic stagnation.

A related factor in the weakening of the PRI was a shift in Mexico's socio-economic structure. Two key reasons the PRI regime had been able to maintain its position of power were stable economic growth and the presence of a large number of peasants directly dependent on the state for survival. However, an unintended consequence of economic growth was the creation of a large middle class. Over time the number of poor peasants in Mexico fell while the number of those in the middle class increased. This growing middle class that characterized Mexico in the 1980s was less dependent on the state and more skeptical of the PRI regime. As a result the regime was able to maintain its grasp on power, but only through increased fraud and political manipulation. Of interest for our study is the role media played both in weakening the PRI's hold on power and the related policy and institutional change that took place.

During the PRI's rule the media played the same role that it does under any authoritarian regime. It was viewed and utilized as a mouthpiece of the ruling elite (Hughes 2006: 50–53). From this standpoint the PRI utilized the media to reinforce the existing institutional equilibria. Broadcasting and advertising contracts were given to those media outlets that provided favorable coverage of the PRI. Further, many political elites owned large stakes in media outlets. It is important to note that most media was not explicitly state owned. Instead the media was largely controlled by private owners who were supporters of the ruling regime. In this manner the media was officially "independent," but in reality was manipulated through the indirect means we discussed in detail in Chapter 3. To be clear, it was not the case that direct government manipulation through state ownership and regulation was completely absent. Instead the preferred means of manipulation was through indirect means such as family ownership of

the media, bribes, lucrative contracts, state ownership of key media infrastructure, and other financial pressures, such as tax breaks and discounts
for use of the state-operated news agency, Notimex.

To provide some concrete examples of this, consider the following.
Government advertising contracts accounted for about half of all advertising revenue for the Mexican print media and were the main source of
advertising revenues for broadcast media. From the 1930s until the 1990s
the production of newsprint remained under the monopolistic control of
the government company PIPSA. During the administration of President
Carlos Salinas, a member of the PRI party, the owner of a major paper—
Unomásuno—was "convinced" by the president's administration to sell
the paper to an owner more sympathetic to the Salinas regime. Salinas
also privatized a previously state-owned television network but demanded
that his older brother, Raúl Salinas, be a silent partner. Along similar lines
Salinas awarded most of the main radio contracts during his presidency to
his brother Raúl, who operated several stations (Lawson 2002: 30–33).

The array of indirect government interventions in the media allowed the
PRI to use the media to coordinate Mexican citizens around its policies.
As such the media played a central role in reinforcing the PRI's rule, which
was a key factor in its sustainability over several decades. To understand
the evolution of the independence of Mexico's media, it is important to
reiterate that while the state was involved in the media through indirect
means, independent media outlets could and did exist and sustain as long
as they did not openly criticize the PRI. Of course there were very few truly
independent media outlets, given the reliance on government advertising
revenues and other financial pressures associated with the government.
But the key is that there was some space for the introduction of alternative
ideas and perceptions, ingredients critical for any policy and institutional
change.

The Rise of Media Independence in Mexico

In his detailed analysis of the rise of Mexican media, Chappell Lawson
(2002: 67–91) provides several key reasons for the emergence of press
independence between the mid-1970s and the late 1990s. One factor was
the presence of a grassroots movement, starting in the early 1970s, of
journalists who desired to provide more balanced reporting, including
open criticisms of the ruling regime. The newspaper *Excélsior* had been
the main outlet for this type of reporting in the 1970s but the government
replaced the paper's editorial board with a more pro-government staff in
the late 1970s (Hughes 2006: 83; Lawson 2002: 66–67). Upon being forced
out of their positions at *Excélsior*, the editors started other independent

publications over the next several years throughout Mexico. The most successful was *Proceso*, which became Mexico's main news-oriented magazine. The numerous publications that the former members of the *Excélsior* started provided the foundation for Mexico's increased media independence. This also contributed to the preference gap between the status quo and the private preferences of Mexican citizens. Many of these independent publications were smaller and lacked the impact of the major media outlets. Nonetheless they did provide some space for alternative ideas and perceptions.

The aforementioned economic downturn in the 1980s and the resulting reforms were another key factor in media independence. The liberalization reforms influenced press independence on two fronts. First, liberalization influenced the economic and political environment facing media outlets. Recall that the reforms included major macroeconomic and microeconomic changes, contributing to a relatively improved environment for business and entrepreneurship. Increased liberalization allowed media outlets greater independence in expanding their operations and seeking alternative sources of financing while simultaneously increasing competition in the broader media industry. As Hughes notes, "political and economic liberalization . . . unleashed a second wave of newspaper transformations based on a diffusion of innovation from the civic-oriented core" (2006: 40). Second, consumers started to demand more coverage of reforms and changes in the political and economic realms. In relation to the gradual effect of media, the increased demand for alternative information contributed to marginal changes in existing institutions and policies and further contributed to the growing gap between citizens' preferences and the status quo. At the same time the media served to reinforce the reforms that had already taken place.

It is important to keep in mind that the PRI continued to control all key forms of government through 1997. The motivation behind many of the economic reforms undertaken under President Salinas was to allow the PRI to continue to maintain its position of power in the face of the economic downturn and call for reforms by the public. Nonetheless the liberalization following the downturn did have an effect in the two aspects discussed above. In the context of media, the reforms expanded the space available for it to introduce alternative perceptions and ideas, resulting in gradual policy and institutional changes, as well as the reinforcement of those changes.

Yet another factor identified by Lawson was changes in journalist norms. During the 1970–1977 period there was a shift in journalist norms toward true independence, separate from direct and indirect state manipulation. Part of this shift can be linked to the economic collapse of the 1980s.

Because of the media's reliance on government for financial support, the downturn and national bankruptcy in the early 1980s forced many media outlets to become less dependent on the government. This is not to say that government influence and support fell to zero. Far from it; the government continued to remain actively involved in the media industry, mainly through indirect manipulation. Nonetheless the economic crisis led to the realization by many journalists and media employees that government involvement was not a guarantee of sustainability and financial success.

Recall that a central part of the reforms under Salinas was the opening of Mexico's borders to trade and investment. The influence from abroad also affected journalistic standards and norms in Mexico. Several key Mexican journalists spent time in the United States and Europe. During their time abroad these journalists observed the journalistic practices and ethics in these other countries and brought them home to Mexico. To some degree the norms present in other countries were imported into Mexico and influenced domestic journalistic standards and norms. In addition to Mexican journalists spending time in other countries, the economic liberalization opened up Mexican borders to outside sources of information. As Hughes notes, "liberalizing trade increased flows of information from abroad, which, in turn, made more journalists come into contact with information that shook tacit understandings of the world" (2006: 41). These external influences exposed Mexican media outlets, and hence Mexican citizens, to alternative sources of information as well as alternative views of media organization and reporting.

International media also played a role in Mexico through partnerships with domestic broadcasting corporations. For example, the American-based National Broadcasting Corporation (NBC) invested in Televisión Azteca following its privatization in 1993. In addition to financial support, NBC also provided news programming and other services to Azteca and was a key factor in making the company commercially viable after years of reliance on state funding.

Increased competition between newspapers and media outlets, coupled with the growth of a strong private advertising sector, also contributed to media independence. For several decades, the PRI had been effective in silencing strong critics of its policies and actions. Starting with the previously discussed *Excélsior* in the 1970s, independent publications critical of the government began to emerge. The number of publications increased throughout the 1980s, and by the 1990s a large number of critical and self-sufficient independent publications had emerged. These papers relied solely on private subscriptions and advertising to finance their operations. To provide some insight into the growth of private advertising, consider Figure 5.1.

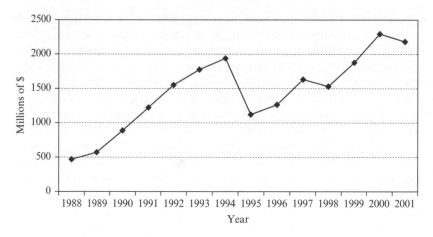

Source: Hughes (2006: 116)

Figure 5.1 *Growth of private sector advertising investment in Mexico,*
1988–2001

As this figure indicates, investment in private advertising grew significantly between 1988 and 2001. The increase in private advertisement was
the result of the economic liberalization discussed above, but also strong
consumer demand for independent reporting. The development of the
private advertising industry had the dual effect of removing the dependence of media outlets on government contracts and subsidies while simultaneously increasing the number of independent publications that entered
the market. Along these lines, Lawson notes, "in a sort of cascade effect,
the initial success of independent publications encouraged the gradual
transformation of the press as a whole" (2002: 89). This transformation
reinforced the changes that had already taken place while simultaneously
contributing to the growing gap between the preferences of Mexican citizens and the status quo.

As mentioned, between the 1930s and the 1990s, the size of Mexico's
middle class grew. This was also a contributing factor to independent
media outlets' ability to sustain themselves without government support.
The increase in the middle class meant increases in literacy and education
and the associated demand for information. The result was a larger market
for news media and hence increased demand for related media products.
This in turn led to increased exposure to alternative perceptions and ideas,
resulting not only in the reinforcement of already adopted reforms but
also in subsequent changes to policies and institutions.

Within the broad Mexican media landscape, the emergence of an independent print media occurred first due to the array of factors discussed above. Although the PRI was able to maintain its influence over the broadcast media (that is, radio and television) for a longer period as compared to the print media, increased independence in the broadcasting sectors soon followed as well. We have traced the unique set of circumstances leading to increased media independence in Mexico. But what was the result of media on Mexico's policies and institutions?

The Impact of Media on Mexico's Policies and Institutions

As the Mexican media became increasingly independent, so too did the diversity of topics and viewpoints reported. As discussed earlier, the Mexican media was viewed by the PRI as a tool for legitimizing its policies and actions. Instead of providing a solution to the Reformers' Dilemma, the PRI viewed the media as a means to reinforce the equilibrium of defection. With the rise of media independence and opposition voices, this became increasingly difficult. More specifically, as the gap between the private preferences of Mexican citizens and the status quo increased, the PRI's grasp on control weakened.

In his analysis of the rise of Mexico's independent press Lawson (2002: 126) makes the distinction between the "old regime" framing of politics and the "civic framing" of politics. The former refers to the political regime under the PRI. The old regime views the political apparatus as a means of rent seeking and corruption benefiting the ruling elite. From this viewpoint, media is a tool to reinforce the status quo and prevent movement away from the existing equilibrium. Civic framing, in contrast, provides the opposite view. It is committed to critical discourse regarding the existing regime, as well as alternative ideologies, institutions, and regimes. It views politics as positive sum in nature, benefiting the citizens of a country at large instead of the benefits accruing to a small segment of the population. In other words, the civic framing view emphasizes policies and institutions as continually evolving and recognizes the media as an important means of discourse in this process.

According to Lawson, the rise of an independent media in Mexico led to a decrease in old regime coverage and an increase in civic discourse. To see this more explicitly consider Figure 5.2. This shows the coverage of old regime discourse versus civic discourse in two of Mexico's main periodicals, *Proceso* and *La Jornada*, during 1984–1996. As the figure illustrates, the percentage of old regime coverage was significantly less than the percentage of coverage dedicated to civic discourse. This highlights a broader shift in media coverage throughout the Mexican media (see Hughes 2006: 76–78).

As further evidence of this point consider Figure 5.3. This shows the

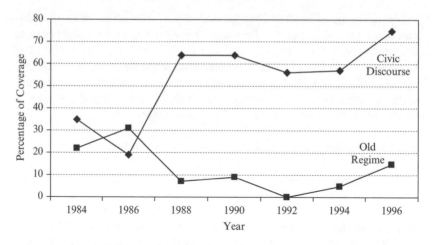

Source: Lawson (2002: 129)

Figure 5.2   Civic and old regime framings of politics in Proceso *and* La
            Jornada, *1984–1996*

amount of time devoted to coverage of officialdom, as a percentage of
total news coverage, on Televisa's popular news show *24 Hours*. Televisa
is one of the major broadcasting companies in Mexico and *24 Hours* is
one of its main news programs. As the figure indicates, the percentage of
programming dedicated to officialdom fell significantly over this decade.
This can be attributed to the increases in media independence discussed
earlier, as well as increases in media outlet competition. Eventually many
aspects of the television industry were privatized, leading to increased
competition and an increase in the diversity of coverage by media outlets
in order to maintain and increase market share (Lawson 2002: 105–106).
This change is reflected in the decrease in the coverage of the government
and PRI as a percentage of total coverage by *24 Hours*, which was facing
increasing competitive pressure from a new evening newscast, Televisión
Azteca's *Hechos de la Noche* (Hughes 2006: 155). This competition forced
established media outlets, which had traditionally been sympathetic
mouthpieces of the state, to diversify their coverage. It also reflects the fact
that Mexican citizens were demanding alternative views and perceptions
instead of simply accepting the status quo.

Government corruption had been a central issue in Mexico for decades.
The increase in media independence served to check some of this corruption. We discussed the role of media as a monitoring device on government in previous chapters and this dynamic is clearly at play in Mexico.

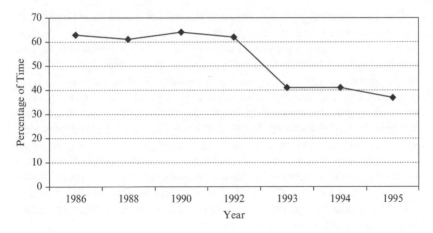

Source: Lawson (2002: 107)

Figure 5.3 Percentage of time devoted to officialdom on Televisa's 24 Hours—1986–1995

Following the rise of media independence in Mexico, the media started to cover such topics as corruption, drug trafficking, political and election fraud, and intimidation.

As a specific example of this, consider the killing of political activists in Guerrero, Mexico, in 1995 by state police. The media engaged in continued investigative journalism and reporting on this story and eventually Guerrero's governor and numerous other state officials were tried for the murders. Local violence against political opposition and activists has been common for decades, but in this case the media served as a monitoring device facilitating the punishment of government officials.

At the national level the media exposed the inner workings of the political apparatus and the channels through which the PRI utilized that apparatus to benefit its members at the expense of Mexican citizens. For example, in the 1990s the media reported on numerous scandals involving various members of the government and linked the web of corruption back to Raúl Salinas, the older brother of Mexican President Carlos Salinas. The investigation of Raúl Salinas's financial dealings was used by the political opposition, which further brought attention not only to the corruption of the incumbent regime but also to the workings of the political system as a whole. The repetition of these stories by numerous media outlets generated common knowledge around the rampant corruption, which served to delegitimize the PRI. In this role the media was critical in activating the tipping point necessary for a punctuated change in institutions.

One can see clear parallels between the role of media in exposing corruption in Mexico and the story that opened this book about corruption in Peru. In both cases the media served as a check on political actors by monitoring their behavior. In addition to making corruption public, the media served to generate common knowledge among citizens. Citizens were well aware that corruption existed throughout the Mexican government. But until the media exposed the corruption, the exact nature and magnitude were not known. Further, even though individual citizens were aware of the corruption, they were unsure what others knew. In other words common knowledge was lacking until media exposed the inner workings of the government. As the media continued to report on the government, it led to the erosion of public support for the PRI. Citizens could be confident that others also knew about the corruption and acted in a concerted effort to generate change.

This erosion of public support culminated in the PRI's loss of the legislative elections in July 1997. Largely because of media monitoring and pressure, the 1997 elections were considered the fairest in Mexico in decades. In 2000 Vicente Fox of the National Action Party (PAN) was elected President of Mexico, marking the first time the PRI had lost a presidential election since its formation in 1929. Felipe Calderón, another PAN candidate, succeeded Fox in 2006 as President of the country. The media played a major role in this shift of power after decades of control by the PRI. More specifically the media facilitated a series of gradual changes which culminated in a punctuated equilibrium involving increased electoral competition and the ultimate removal of the PRI from power. The punctuated equilibrium in Mexico did not result in a collapse or wholesale change in institutions. Instead it involved the removal of the PRI's dominant grasp on power, which had existed for several decades.

Summation

The case of Mexico illuminates the Reformers' Dilemma framework, as well as many of the mechanisms discussed throughout this book. For decades the Mexican media was used as a tool by the ruling elite to maintain and bolster support for its policies and activities according to the reinforcement effect discussed in Chapter 1. Government's interventions in the media provides an important illustration of the indirect forms of media manipulation discussed in detail in Chapter 3. The PRI's use of media to maintain its system of corruption and rent seeking also illuminates the Reformers' Dilemma as illustrated in Figure 2.2 of Chapter 2. In the absence of a coordination-enhancing mechanism, political officials have the incentive to defect by catering to private and special interests. This was the case under the PRI prior to the emergence of a media strong enough to check the government.

Due to an array of exogenous factors—the economic downturn and national bankruptcy, changes in journalistic norms and standards and the rise of a middle class—the independence of Mexico's media increased over time. This allowed the media to generate gradual change and the common knowledge required to activate the tipping point necessary for a new punctuated equilibrium. This punctuated change consisted of the removal of the PRI from its dominant position of power.

Although Mexico's economic downturn operated to help propel improved media freedom when media outlets were forced to seek outside, private financing instead of turning to the now bankrupt government for this purpose, as we discuss in our next case study on Russia, economic crisis need not carry this silver lining in terms of media dependence. In particular, another potential response to economic trouble is for media outlets to seek additional state support to continue to run, increasing their reliance on the state. As we discussed above, this was not a viable option in Mexico where government was bankrupt. However, as we will explore below, in the case of Russia, economic downturn had precisely the opposite effect on media independence.

The exogenous factors that spurred increased media freedom in Mexico also highlight a more general point. The emergence of the process of media freedom is often the result of some exogenous shock to the broader political, economic, and social system. However, once the forces of media independence are set in motion, the case of Mexico indicates that they can be self-sustaining and self-extending and facilitate a solution to the Reformers' Dilemma. As Lawson notes,

> the Mexican experience calls attention to the mutually reinforcing relationship between changes in the mass media and changes in other elements of a political system. Scholars of regime change cannot assume that the media will act as a 'caboose of the state.' Given market competition and the emergence of new journalistic norms, they [the media] can also be a locomotive of change (2002: 181).

An interesting aspect of the Mexican case is that political officials did not actively adopt policies to increase media independence and freedom. Instead media independence increased despite indirect government intervention in the media industry and direct government intervention in many other industries throughout the country. Even with a relatively small space to act freely, media played an important role in reinforcing reforms and serving as a catalyst of subsequent changes.

The influence of external media influences, both in terms of journalistic standards and foreign partnerships and investment, illustrates our discussion of the importance of allowing free exchange and trade with foreign media and foreign investors. The experience of Mexican journalists in developed countries exposed them to different models of media reporting and management, and foreign investment was critical in supporting previously state-financed media outlets. When a country opens its borders to foreign media, it allows for the imitation of existing standards and techniques (for example, journalistic standards, reporting techniques and management techniques) while simultaneously expanding the menu of media products and services offered to citizens.

We do not want to oversell the extent of media freedom in Mexico. Freedom House (2007) currently ranks Mexico's media as "partially free." Issues such as violence against journalists and state-level defamation laws remain major concerns. However, when compared to the preceding decades, the media freedom that emerged in Mexico starting in the 1980s is quite remarkable. Also significant is the impact that the increase in media independence had on Mexican political and social outcomes, as illustrated by the electoral losses of the PRI in the later 1990s.

It also remains to be seen whether the changes that have occurred in Mexico since this time will become reinforced over a longer period. Political corruption continues to be a problem, but the media continues to serve as a monitoring mechanism. For example, in 2004 three videos showing politicians engaged in bribery and questionable behavior were aired on Mexican television. One video showed René Bejarano, a Mexico City assemblyman, accepting a bribe from a city contractor. Another video showed the President of the Mexican Green Party, the fourth largest political party in Mexico, discussing a payment for his party's support of proposed zoning changes in Cancún. The third video showed the Mexico City finance secretary gambling thousands of dollars in a Las Vegas casino (Hughes 2006: 186–187). Despite the ongoing issues and concerns, the case of Mexico clearly illustrates the power of media to check political officials and serve as a catalyst of policy and institutional change.

RUSSIA

Historical Background of the Russian Media

Russian media has a long history that can be traced back over several centuries. For the purposes of our analysis, the main period of interest begins in the early 1920s with the rise of the Soviet Union. Newspapers played a central role in the Soviet propaganda system. Radio, television, and the cinema were also important parts of that system, but newspapers were the key means of communication.

Understanding the ability of media to effectively coordinate a large number of people, Lenin placed controls on the press following the Bolshevik Revolution. He viewed newspapers as tools for collectivist propaganda and organization (Hollander 1972; Turpin 1995). Stalin and Khrushchev continued Lenin's legacy and utilized the media to communicate official news, educate and instill ideology, and present an idealized view of life in the Soviet system.

To further understand media's importance in the Soviet system, consider that the Union of Journalists was formed in 1957, and by 1966 membership had increased to 43 000, making it the largest union in the country (Hollander 1972). The purpose of forming the union was so that the state could achieve better control over journalists through centralization. Journalists were provided with clear guidelines for their reporting which included: unconditional party loyalty, patriotism, truthfulness to Leninist theory, and accessibility to the average reader (Hollander 1972). Journalists were closely monitored in their application of these guidelines and were told what topics were acceptable for media coverage.

A complex monitoring system was established to oversee the media. The Chief Administration for Literary and Publishing Affairs was established in 1922 and was later renamed the Chief Administration for the Protection of Military and State Secrets in 1957. This administration's function was to review and approve all printed materials and to monitor all media outlets (Hopkins 1970). There were several other government administrations established to oversee the mass media. For example, the Department of Propaganda was in charge of filling editorial and management positions in the various media outlets throughout the country. To put this in terms of our earlier discussion regarding government manipulation of the media (see Chapter 3), the Soviet media was subject to direct government manipulation through state ownership, censorship, and the direct appointment of media personnel.

Despite official control of mass media, *samizdat*—"self publication"— emerged and was prevalent in the post-Stalin USSR. This involved the underground production and distribution of a wide range of media including political and social commentary, full-length manuscripts on a variety of topics, and art and poetry (Hollander 1972: 183–186). The underground media provided alternative ideas to those the state disseminated through official media. As we discuss below, the underground media played a key role as a catalyst of change in Russia.

It is within this historical context of decades of strict state control that the communist system collapsed. Our goal is twofold. First, we want to understand how the media contributed to the fall of communism. Second, we want to understand if and how the media contributed to the Reformers' Dilemma that existed in Russia. Boettke (1993) characterizes the Soviet system as a rent-seeking society with the main goal of generating perquisites for the ruling elite. The system of interlocked monopolies benefited those in power and because of this the elite had a direct interest in maintaining the system. This posed a problem for reforms because, as Boettke (1993: 6) notes, "reform demanded a change in this way of doing things, but change was sure to be resisted" by those who had a vested interest in the status quo. In the context of the Reformers' Dilemma, reformers had an incentive to pursue their own private interests at the expense of Russian citizens. In theory increased media freedom could overcome this problem and serve as a solution to the Reformers' Dilemma.

The Rise and Fall of Russian Media Independence

The state directly controlled the media from the 1920s. However, an underground media—*samizdat*—emerged in the 1950s. This was an important source of alternative ideas and perceptions and contributed to institutional change. Consider, for example, one of the most popular underground publications, the *Chronicle of Current Events* (*Khronika Tekushchikh Sobytiy*). Published every two months, each issue of the *Chronicle* began with the United Nations General Declaration on Human Rights that all individuals have a right to freedom of convictions and expression. The *Chronicle* was "a clearly defined journal of dissent . . . providing a forum for the exchange of information about political protest" (Hollander 1972: 184). The *Chronicle* and myriad other underground literatures contributed to the gradual divergence between private and public preferences. According to Downing, for example, "*Samizdat* media had no dramatic, instant impact: they represented a gradual burn into the deep fabric of power" (1996: 76). Ultimately this contributed to the potential tipping point—the collapse of communism—resulting in a new punctuated equilibrium.

In addition to this gradual effect on institutions, other factors, such as declining economic conditions and the continued war with Afghanistan, created pressure for reforms. Mikhail Gorbachev, who assumed power in 1985, introduced political reforms (*glasnost*) and economic and social ones (*perestroika* and *uskoreniye*). The goal of the reforms to re-establish the Communist Party's power by addressing the growing dissent resulting from the aforementioned factors.

Changes in existing media laws were a key aspect of these reforms (Mickiewicz 2000: 94–98). In August 1990 the Russian government created a media law that provided a foundation for free speech and expression. The law prohibited censorship and barred government from shutting down media outlets (for example, newspapers and broadcasting outlets) except by court order. It also provided a formal process for registering newspapers and broadcasting. This allowed much of the media to move above ground, which was critical to the punctuated institutional change that occurred shortly thereafter. As in Mexico, this chain of events highlights the importance of outside factors in influencing media's three effects. According to Sparks, "The media was able to take advantage of this opening [created by the reforms] to act more independently" (1998: 14). Indeed, because of the space these changes in media laws associated with broader reform created, media contributed to a new punctuated equilibrium.

The freed media critically reported on Soviet economic, political, and social circumstances. Although the underground media had long addressed these issues, the above-ground media had a greater reach, making it a more effective common knowledge creator. "Newspaper editors . . . distinguished their papers from the standardized fare" by publishing "stories sharply critical of the armed forces, the KGB, and previous Soviet regimes" (Mickiewicz 2000: 96). Media-created common knowledge of dissent accelerated movement toward a tipping point for punctuated institutional change. By 1990 government had lost much of its power over the economy, social networks, and associations. The 1991 coup attempt by members of the Communist Party revealed the instability of existing political institutions. A series of USSR member state referendums on independence led to the Soviet Union's dissolution in 1991. Russian media played an important role in contributing to the gradual divergence of private and public preferences and in realizing a new punctuated equilibrium in 1991. Eroding economic, political, and social conditions were important factors giving media the space to create the common knowledge required to activate the tipping point necessary for this change.

Boris Yeltsin signed a subsequent media law in December 1991. This law overlapped with the 1990 law in many aspects. For example, the subsequent law reiterated the ban on censorship as well as the registration process for media outlets. The 1991 law called for the establishment of a Federal Commission for Television and Radio to oversee the registration process. It also provided some boundaries on the limits of free speech, including the disclosure of protected state secrets, intolerance, and attempts to overthrow the political system by force (Benn 1996: 472).

During Yeltsin's early years in office, the independent media continued to flourish. Describing this period, Zassoursky notes that "throughout the final years of the Gorbachev administration and during the first years under Yeltsin, the press was a genuinely independent institution and, in an environment of weak political authority and a chaotic economy, had enormous power" (2004: 16). However, this period of media independence was short lived.

The main reason media freedom was eroded was that the media was never fully institutionalized as an independent entity. Although the 1990 and 1991 media laws provided a framework for media independence and freedom of expression, there was never a clean break between the Russian media and the Russian political system. The concept of the media as the "fourth estate" holds that media should be an independent and self-sustaining institution that stands separate from the legislative, executive, and judicial branches (Zassoursky 2004: 11). In Russia the media as a fourth estate never emerged since it remained closely intertwined with the political apparatus, just as it had in the preceding decades.

The economic downturn that occurred in Russia in the early 1990s was one reason for this outcome. To characterize the scope of this downturn, consider that per capita income fell by more than 50 per cent over a decade. Between 1990 and 1999 Russia's average annual decline in GDP was 6.1 per cent (Carrington and Nelson 2002: 236–237). In the context of the media, the downturn was important because independent media outlets had a difficult time becoming financially independent. To understand the difficulties facing some of the most popular papers consider the changes in print runs during 1991–1995. The print run of *Izvestiya* fell from 4 700 000 to 811 000 while the print run for *Pravda* declined from 2 628 000 to about 204 000. Well-known weekly publications also suffered. The print run of the *Literaturnaya gazetta* fell from 1 200 000 to 325 000 while the print-run of the *Argumenty i fakty* declined from 24 527 000 to 4 200 000 (Benn 1996: 474).

The economic downturn, coupled with the ineffectiveness of reforms and uncertainty regarding the general "rules of the game" governing economic interactions, made it difficult to attract foreign investment. As Chapter 3 (see Figure 3.3) discussed, an advertising industry capable of supporting an independent press failed to emerge in Russia. The response by many media outlets was to turn to the government for financial support. The result was that the media outlets never became truly independent of political dependence and influence.

The continuing media dependence on government posed a problem. On the one hand media outlets wanted to maintain their journalistic and editorial independence while receiving continued support from the government. On the other hand many government officials wanted the media to refrain from criticizing government or to provide favorable coverage in exchange for ongoing financial support. Discussing this tension, Elena Androunas writes, "Under the communists, the press pretended that it was free of ideological pressure. Now it pretends that it can be free of pressure from the government while being supported by government subsidies" (1993: 63). As noted earlier, throughout the history of the Soviet Union, the main form of government manipulation of media was direct influence through state ownership, direct censorship, and the direct appointment of journalists and media employees. Government financing and bailouts during the economic downturn of the 1990s shifted the form of government manipulation from direct to indirect, but not the fact that government manipulation still existed.

Because of the continued reliance on government financing, media was never able to escape its past and break with the political system. The Soviet-system media was viewed and used as a key part of the broader propaganda system. Further, the rent-seeking nature of the Soviet system made reforms difficult because any attempted reform had to deal with the problem of vested interests that resisted such changes, as captured by the Reformers' Dilemma. As media outlets simultaneously sought independence and continued government support, they remained trapped within the existing system. The ruling elite continued to provide financial support to media outlets with the expectation of reciprocation in the form of positive media coverage that would allow rulers to maintain their positions of power.

The close linkages between the political system and media continued even after the implementation of the 1990 and 1991 media laws, which temporarily provided a framework for media independence. As Zassoursky notes, "at the height of the economic crisis of 1992, the alliance between the government and the 'democratic' mass media . . . became even closer thanks to the development of a system of subsidies and economic assistance" (2004: 16). The government provided subsidies through reimbursements for production, price fixing of the paper used in production, forgiving and paying down the debts of media outlets, and transferring ownership of buildings and other infrastructure to media outlets.

To provide a better understanding of the continued link between the Russian political system and media, consider the case of ORT.[1] The founding of ORT can be traced back to 1994 and marks the beginning of the well-known oligarch Boris Berezovsky's media holding company.[2] This was formed after it was decided by President Yeltsin's family that a favorable news environment was needed for the upcoming presidential elections in the spring of 1996 (Zassoursky 2004: 28). Berezovsky was given a 49 per cent stake in ORT and in order to finance the operations of the media outlet, the government sold him shares in the oil company Sibneft well below book value. ORT, along with the other media outlets connected to Yeltsin, provided strong support during his re-election campaign, which proved successful, as Yeltsin was re-elected to office. The positive relationship between Berezovsky and Yeltsin continued after the president's re-election, when Berezovsky was sold shares in other previously state-owned businesses below market value.

The case of ORT is important for several reasons. It illuminates the nature of the relationship between the political system and much of the media in Russia. Even when media outlets were "privatized," there was still significant government manipulation through indirect means. These pseudo-privatizations continued the rent-seeking society that had existed for decades, albeit in a different form. Colin Sparks captures the fact that little had changed when he writes,

> The media before the fall of communism were large-scale, hierarchically organized, bureaucratic establishments in which there were elaborate procedures for ensuring acquiescence to the will of the directorate. The media after the fall of communism are large-scale, hierarchically organized, bureaucratic establishments in which there are elaborate procedures for ensuring acquiescence to the will of the directorate (2000: 45).

A key difference in the post-communist period is the role oligarchs played in running the media. As the case of ORT illustrates, many major media outlets were privatized through political ties with the expectation that they would benefit politicians via favorable coverage.

The case of ORT also highlights the fragility of the relationships between political leaders and oligarchs. Absent institutionalized checks and balances to create a media independent from government manipulation, media outlets and their oligarch owners were subject to changes in political leadership and changes in relationships with political leaders. This became evident in the case of Boris Berezovsky and ORT in early 2000 (Becker 2004: 151). ORT originally backed Vladimir Putin during his 2000 campaign for the Russian presidency, which he won. However, ORT became more critical of Putin over a number of issues including the President's handling of the Kursk submarine disaster. In 2001 Berezovsky claimed he was threatened by the government with jail time for improper financial dealings if he refused to sell his 49 per cent stake in ORT to a buyer sympathetic to the Kremlin. Since relinquishing his shares in ORT, Berezovsky has become an outspoken critic of Putin and an advocate, at least in rhetoric, of political and economic liberalization in Russia. Ironically many of Berezovsky's Russian business interests are not the result of genuine capitalism but instead of crony capitalism whereby privileges are given to those with political connections. This is far from true economic liberalization.

Another oligarch, Vladimir Gusinsky, had an experience similar to Berezovsky's. Gusinsky was the founder of the Most-Media holding group, which included Most Bank, the NTV channel, and the *Segodnya* newspaper, as well as several magazines. Gusinsky had close political ties to Yuri Luzhkov, the Mayor of Moscow, who helped him secure ownership of some of the major media enterprises constituting Most-Media. NTV was one of the first independent television stations in Russia and attracted leading journalists and reporters from state-operated media outlets. Similar to Berezovsky's ORT, NTV was a major supporter of Yeltsin in the 1996 re-election campaign and Gusinsky and Yeltsin remained on good terms throughout Yeltsin's presidency. However, in 1999 NTV was critical of the Russian government's involvement in the Chechen wars and of the policies of Vladimir Putin. Following Putin's election in 2000 he exacted revenge on Gusinsky and Media-Most holdings. This included selective use of tax and criminal laws to arrest and charge Gusinsky (Becker 2004: 151). The charges against Gusinsky were dropped, but only after he agreed to sell his share in NTV to the government-controlled Gazprom (Becker 2004: 152). In April 2001 Gazprom officially took over NTV and replaced the management and journalistic team with employees more sympathetic to Putin.

The cases of ORT and NTV illustrate the close connection between the Russian political system and the Russian media. They also illuminate the fragility of the relationships between political elites and oligarchs. In both cases the media was intertwined with the political system, allowing government manipulation through both direct and indirect means. The Russian media was never able to overcome its dependence on the government and hence was never able to facilitate a sustainable solution to the Reformers' Dilemma.

The Impact of Media on Russia's Policies and Institutions

Media played a key role in communism's collapse. The underground media contributed to gradual change in institutions and the independent media that existed in the early 1990s contributed to the new punctuated institutional equilibrium. However, media failed to solve the Reformers' Dilemma facing the Soviet Union during the *glasnost* period and Russia after communism's collapse. Media independence was fleeting and whatever strides were made in media freedom were quickly eroded. Thus the media had little to no sustainable impact on the adoption of beneficial reforms in Russia. Instead the media continues to be manipulated by those in the Russian government to subvert reforms and maintain their positions of power. Instead of providing a solution to the Reformers' Dilemma, the media continues to be used as a tool to maintain the status quo. Private interests are pursued at the expense of the broader interests of Russian citizens. Considering the state of the Russian media since 2000 illuminates why it has been ineffective in overcoming the Reformers' Dilemma.

In September 2000 President Vladimir Putin signed the Information Security Doctrine, which was the foundation of the government's new policy toward media. The document expressed a commitment to press freedom and indicated that state monopolization of media was prohibited. However, the document also left much room for government manipulation. While calling for increased media freedom, the doctrine also called for a halt to foreign investment in media, as well as the need to further develop state-operated media and a pool of loyal journalists.

The actions of the Putin government seem to cut directly against the rhetoric of press freedom found in the Information Security Doctrine. Consider for instance that Putin travels with a handpicked group of reporters. Most of these reporters work for the state and those that raise unwanted questions are replaced in the pool. Many broadcasts shown on television are influenced and approved by the Kremlin (Baker 2005). Indeed Russia's three major television networks—Channel Russia, ORT and NTV—are either directly controlled by the state or are in the hands of individuals who are loyal to Putin and his administration.[3]

It is important to note that explicit state ownership of the media has actually fallen under Putin. For example, as of 2006 the state's share of direct ownership in the newspaper and journal market was estimated at around 10 per cent. The overall number of registered periodicals has also increased under Putin from 21 000 in 1997 to 58 000 in 2007 (Petro 2007). However, these changes must be interpreted in context. First, they fail to capture the indirect means through which the government manipulates the media. Further, as we discuss in more detail below, the appearance of independence in printed media is part of Putin's attempt to create a "managed democracy." Central to this effort is state control of television broadcasting but some semblance of independence in print media (Lipman and McFaul 2001: 116).

According to Freedom House's *Freedom of the Press* report, overall media freedom has fallen since Putin has been in office. Freedom House downgraded Russia's overall media score to "not free" starting in 2002 and its overall rating has remained in that category since then. Government authorities at all levels employ both direct and indirect pressures to manipulate the media. Media outlets throughout Russia remain dependent on government subsidies and other forms of financial favoritism (Carrington and Nelson 2002: 237). The coercion of journalists is yet another major issue. Russia remains one of the deadliest countries in the world for journalists. According to Reporters Sans Frontières (2007), 21 journalists have been killed in Russia since Putin came to power in 2000. Even well-known journalists are not immune to the threat of coercion, as illustrated by the October 2006 murder of reporter Anna Politkovskaya, who worked for the weekly *Novaya Gazeta*. Politkovskaya had been a strong critic of the Putin administration, as well as Russia's actions in the Chechen conflict. Her murder has yet to be solved but the circumstances surrounding her death are suspicious.

Becker (2004) characterizes the Russian media under Putin as "neo-authoritarian." Under such a system pluralism in the media is acceptable but only up to a point. There are clear limits on the media, especially when it comes to issues associated with the actions of the government (for example, government interventions abroad, major domestic government initiatives, corruption, and elections). Under neo-authoritarian systems, those in political power use the media as a weapon against political opposition (Belin 2001; Becker 2004). Further, within such a system the government typically relies on indirect means of government control and manipulation. These include, but are not limited to, control of entry through licensing and regulation, subsidies, advertising contracts, tax and debt breaks, and the use of ambiguous laws and regulations to punish journalists and media owners and employees (Becker 2002: 168–170 and Becker 2004: 149–150). All of these indirect forms of government manipulation have been employed in Russia.

A key difference between neo-authoritarian and more traditional authoritarian regimes is that the former allow and tolerate elements of independent media to give the appearance of a commitment to democracy. Such regimes typically aim to control television broadcasting because it is traditionally considered to be the most important and effective form of media communication (Becker 2004: 150). As discussed above, the Kremlin either directly controls, or has sympathetic individuals controlling, the three major Russian broadcasting outlets. This allows for the creation of a "managed democracy" whereby the ruling elite attempt to project the image of liberal democratic institutions while simultaneously exerting control and influence over those institutions so as to maintain their hold on power. Elements of independence exist but with strong constraints on how that independence can be exercised. Such control over the media renders it useless as a solution to the Reformers' Dilemma.

Summation

The case of Russia provides several important insights for our analysis. First, it highlights the three effects of media discussed in Chapter 1.

Starting in the 1920s, the state attempted to use the media to reinforce the status quo. However, the emergence of an underground media in the 1950s led to a gradual divergence between private preferences and the existing institutional equilibria. In the early 1990s media played an important role in realizing a new punctuated equilibrium.

Like Mexico, the case of Russia illustrates how exogenous factors can influence media and its three effects on policies and institutions. In the case of Russia, eroding economic, political, and social conditions were important factors giving media the space to create the common knowledge required to activate the tipping point necessary for change.

Russia also provides insight into our analysis of media as a solution to the Reformers' Dilemma. There was some effort, in the form of the 1990 and 1991 media laws, to create space for a free and independent media. However, the media was never able to escape the political system. As we discussed, part of this was due to the economic downturn in the early 1990s. Russia illustrates the opposite response media may have to economic collapse, which contrasts strongly with the response in Mexico discussed above. In Russia, in the wake of economic downturn, many media outlets turned to the government for financial support, which prevented them from achieving true independence and undermined media freedom. Thus severe economic recession can be helpful (as in the case of Mexico) or harmful (as in the case of Russia) to media independence and thus to a solution to the Reformers' Dilemma depending upon how media outlets respond to the crisis and the nature of the downturn, which impacts government's ability to support media seeking financial support.

Another significant insight provided by the Russian case is the important distinction between capitalism and crony capitalism. Capitalism is a system of social and economic organization based on private property, free markets, entrepreneurship, competition, and free entry and exit. Crony capitalism, in contrast, is a system whereby individuals use political connections to secure favorable positions. These may include government-granted monopolies through licensing or regulation, favorable tax laws and subsidies, or ownership stakes in a previously state-owned asset. Under such a system the allocation of resources is not based on competition and free exchange but instead on the existence of political ties and the ability of individuals to utilize those ties to their advantage. As we saw in the case of Russia, the means of privatizing many state-owned media outlets involved reliance on political ties. Recall, for instance, that Boris Berezovsky secured an ownership stake in ORT, among other state-owned assets, through his connections with Boris Yeltsin and his willingness to use ORT to support Yeltsin's 1996 re-election campaign. This method of privatization failed to sever the connection between media and the political system and prevented the media from achieving the freedom necessary for it to be a solution to the Reformers' Dilemma.

Crony capitalism clearly defeats the aim of privatizing the media—to remove it from political influences—since such a system is grounded, by its very nature, in political connections. This raises an important question: How are media assets to be allocated to avoid the negative consequences associated with crony capitalism? This is especially important in developing and transition countries where political ties typically have a long history of being important for daily survival.

The first-best means of allocating media assets is to auction off all of the state-owned assets in a completely open auction.[4] Ideally the auction should be open to both domestic and foreign investors and the assets should be awarded to the bidder with the highest cash bid. Privatization efforts that sell only part of the assets, limit auctions to a small number of bidders, or attempt to place conditions on bidders based on the quality of bidder, quality of business plans, or promises of future investment, should be avoided because this creates opportunity for political manipulation (Anderson 2004: 96–120). An open, unconditional auction is the best means for allocating resources to those that value them the most while simultaneously overcoming the problems associated with crony capitalism. Anderson notes that when this method is used "there is little discretion on the part of the privatization officials and thus little chance that they can be accused of favoritism or corruption in selecting the winner" (Anderson 2004: 97).

Media's history in Russia also serves to provide examples of the various forms of government media manipulation discussed in Chapter 3. Russian media under the Soviet system was characterized by direct manipulation through state ownership, censorship, and the direct appointment of journalists and media employees and managers. Following the collapse of the Soviet system, government influence shifted from direct to indirect manipulation. While elements of direct manipulation still exist, the main forms of government influence now include government subsidies, debt forgiveness, advertising contracts, and the allocation of infrastructure from the government to privileged media outlets.

Related to the issue of government manipulation, the case of Russia highlights how the media can be used as a tool by neo-authoritarian regimes. These regimes allow elements of independent media to exist in order to project a commitment to democracy but in reality closely monitor and constrain the behavior of these media outlets. Further, neo-authoritarian regimes exert direct and indirect control over media outlets with the greatest reach and influence. In this context the media acts as a means of reinforcing the Reformers' Dilemma rather than as a solution to this dilemma.

POLAND

Historical Background of Poland's Media

Poland's media can be traced back to 1661 when the country's first newspaper, *Merkuriusz Polski*, appeared as a royal publication. For over a century starting in the late eighteenth century, Poland was controlled by German, Austrian, and Russian autocratic governments. While the specifics of media control differed under each of these regimes, the common theme was that published material was reviewed and censored by the occupying powers. As such, media in Poland had a long history of being directly connected to the political elite, as well as of direct dependence on the political system.

Poland achieved its independence in 1918, but that independence was fleeting. In 1939 the Nazis invaded Poland from the west while the Soviets invaded from the east. Following these successful invasions, control of Poland was divided between the Germans and Russians. Both banned all Polish newspapers, closed existing radio stations, and implemented a system of state-controlled newspapers, as well as loudspeakers throughout their respective zones to communicate news, directives, and propaganda (Goban-Klas 1994: 43–44).

Following World War II and the collapse of the German administration in Poland, a new communist-controlled government, the Polish Committee of National Liberation, emerged in July 1944. A few months later, following the Yalta Agreement in February 1945, a new Polish government was established. The new government was the result of a compromise between the existing communist government and the exiled Polish government.[5] It is important to note that this new provisional government was dominated by members of the communist government. The first postwar elections were held in January 1947. The communists easily won the election, which was considered by many to be fraudulent (see Goban-Klas 1994: 52–53). The communists would maintain their hold on power until 1990.

Following World War II, the government quickly became Poland's biggest publisher. In 1945 a bill limiting private printing of media was introduced and a year later all paper mills and printing plants were nationalized. Soon thereafter the allocation of newsprint and paper was centralized in the hands of the state. By 1949 the state controlled the distribution of all newspapers and magazines (Goban-Klas 1994: 54). The

Ministry of Information and Propaganda had been established in 1944 and continued in operation under the new Polish government. Indeed, the Ministry played a key role in influencing Poland's first postwar elections in 1947 by shutting down or severely restricting most non-communist newspapers. Similar to Russia and other communist regimes, the media played a central role in the sustainability and operation of the government (Naumann 2004: 1). As Goban-Klas notes, "since the late 1940s and early 1950s the [Polish] media policy had two goals: to win support from a hostile population for Communist rule in Poland and to emulate Soviet propaganda" (1994: 73).

Although the 1952 Polish constitution guaranteed freedom of the press, all aspects of the Polish media were controlled by the state. The government trained and appointed journalists and media employees and provided directives to media outlets regarding appropriate topics for coverage. All media stories and editorials were censored and edited by state officials before being published or broadcast. State control of the media covered newspapers, magazines, radio broadcasts, films, popular books, textbooks, stamps, and songs. For the most part the laws and regulations concerning censorship were effective due to the threat of imprisonment or death for deviation from those rules. For example, most journalists were careful to communicate the party line and not come across as critical of the government for fear of punishment.

Since the Polish media system was based on the existing Soviet system, it makes sense that a bureaucracy similar to Russia's was established to monitor and operate the media. Overseeing the entire Polish media was the Department of the Press, Radio and Publications. Beneath this department was a series of agencies and departments for each branch of the media. For example, the Department of Press and Publication oversaw newspapers, while the Ministry of Telecommunications and the Committee for Radiophonization oversaw radio broadcasting. Journalists and media employees were closely monitored and, unlike Mexico, they lacked the opportunity for exposure to external norms and management techniques.

For the next several decades the media remained under the control of the communist government. Changes did occur over that period. For example, in the 1970s under Edward Gierek, television became a central political medium and joined other forms of media under strict government control. The state-run television channels were used to communicate news, directives, and the achievements of the communist system. Over the course of the 1970s, the amount of television broadcasting increased by approximately 60 per cent (Goban-Klas 1994: 149). The state would maintain its hold on all forms of Polish media throughout the decade. During the communist government's hold on power, the "iron rule was that propaganda is more important than butter—although the shops may not have butter, the newspapers still had to be sold on a daily basis" (Goban-Klas 1994: 175). This points to an understanding on the part of government officials of the power of media as a mechanism for widespread coordination.

It is also important to note that, similar to Russia, a robust underground press emerged in Poland in the late 1970s. The previously mentioned phenomenon of *samizdat* was an important aspect of life in Poland. In addition to underground copies of books and pamphlets, weekly and biweekly newspapers were also published. For example, the biweekly paper, *Robotnik*, which first appeared in 1977, aimed to "convey the truth, since the official press did not fulfill this role; on the contrary, it was full of lies and slanders" (quoted in Goban-Klas 1994: 156). Hundreds of other independent papers emerged in the late 1970s covering a wide range of topics. As Millard notes, "the gathering strength of the underground press provided alternative sources of information not only on current politics but also on key events in Polish history and access to literary works frowned upon by the regime" (1998: 88). While the smaller print run of these underground papers could never compete with official government papers, they were a form of independent press that published outside the strict constraints of government censorship.

The underground media gradually facilitated institutional change by contributing to the growing gap between citizens' actual and publicly stated preferences. It created common knowledge around alternative ideas and communicated planned and actual acts of dissent. For example, the underground media played an important role in coordinating worker strikes orchestrated by the Solidarity dissident movement. The gradual effect of marginal institutional changes continued through the late 1980s. For instance, the Gdańsk Agreement of 1980 between workers and government introduced marginal changes, including the formation of civil groups independent of the communist government and increased freedom of speech in printed material. The emergence of underground media signaled that the state could not control all forms of media and foreshadowed the events that would occur starting in the early 1980s.

The Rise of Poland's Media Independence

The Pope's visit to Poland in 1979, coupled with worsening economic conditions and a series of worker strikes in the early 1980s, are typically cited as the beginning of the end of the communist regime in Poland. As mentioned, the underground press had long been a means of communication and coordination for the workers and played a key role in facilitating the strikes. Further, underground media was the main source of alternative perceptions and ideas leading to the gap between worker preferences and the status quo. A series of worker strikes orchestrated by the Solidarity dissident movement led to the aforementioned Gdańsk Agreement between the Polish government and the workers. A key part of the worker demands was the call for freedom of speech in publications. In an attempt to remain in control while accommodating the workers, government met the demands and stated that censorship would only be applied to instances involving state secrets. Although media independence did not occur instantaneously, the content of the Gdańsk Agreement was a major event in the history of Polish media. In theory the terms of the agreement ended the communist party monopoly over the media and provided the foundation for a pluralistic media. This is yet another example of how a largely unfree media can contribute to changes that lead to subsequent reforms and independence for media outlets.

Following the Gdańsk Agreement, the media began investigative reporting on such topics as political events, corruption, and the accuracy of official statistics. During this time,

the traditional roles of the daily and weekly press changed. Dailies began to utilize in-depth reporting and lengthy essays, whereas weeklies kept abreast of ongoing political developments, informing people about the events of the day . . . editorial discussions of formerly forbidden topics were organized and published (Goban-Klas 1994: 169).

In this role media not only served as a check on the government but also introduced citizens to alternative viewpoints and dissenting opinions, further contributing to gradual changes in existing policies and institutions.

In October 1981, thanks to the demands of the striking workers, a new censorship law was passed. This was important because the new formal law allowed government censorship to be challenged through the court system and placed a check on government actors. The law guaranteed freedom of speech and outlined the conditions under which press freedom was restricted.

However, Poland's newfound media independence did not last long. In December 1981 Wojciech Jaruzelski, the Communist Party's new prime minister, declared martial law. Jaruzelski claimed that this law was necessary because the country was on the verge of economic and civil unrest. The decree included an initial crackdown on Solidarity, including the imprisonment of its leaders and eventually the official banning of the union in 1982. In terms of our framework, the imposition of martial law was an attempt to squash the growing divergence between citizen preference for change and the institutional status quo. The government attempted to limit media's ability to be a mechanism of change away from the status quo and instead tried to redirect its use to reinforcing the status quo.

Despite the ban, the Solidarity movement continued its operations underground and remained a powerful and influential force throughout the country. A key part of Solidarity's ongoing efforts and influence was an underground media campaign, including pamphlets, newsletters, and weekly newspapers (Goban-Klas 1994: 187). The declaration of martial law also included the suspension of freedom of speech and introduced new regulations regarding all forms of media and communications. Although martial law remained in place until 1983, the control of the communist regime over the country had weakened significantly, evidenced by the need to issue the decree in the first place, as well as the continued operations of Solidarity and the underground press.

Even during the period of martial law, new forms of media experienced growth. For example, new weeklies were introduced and the Catholic press actually increased its print run, achieving a circulation of over two million. Although the government had a strong hold on traditional television broadcasting, the introduction of videos and camcorders allowed the exchange of videos largely outside the control of government (Goban-Klas 1994: 196). Also important was the introduction of satellite antennas, which allowed Polish citizens to view foreign broadcasts. These changes in technologies significantly weakened the government's monopoly on television broadcasting and information. In doing so they limited the government's efforts to reinforce the status quo by limiting exposure to alternative perceptions and ideas. They also further contributed to the already significant preference gap.

Following another series of worker strikes in 1988, the government came to the realization that to remain in power and implement reforms it was going to have to deal with the still banned, yet heavily influential, Solidarity movement. The government reached out to Lech Wałęsa, the co-founder and leader of Solidarity. In addition to co-founding Solidarity, Wałęsa had been arrested under the declaration of martial law in 1981 and had been awarded the Nobel Peace Prize in 1983 for his efforts against the communist regime. The government's goal was to incorporate Wałęsa as a minor political player in order to accommodate the Solidarity movement and prevent future worker strikes.

As part of this process, a live televised debate between Wałęsa and Alfred Miodowicz—the president of the state trade unions—was held to discuss the pressing problems facing the country. In this regard the media proved critical in activating the tipping point created by the large preference gap—itself largely the product of Poland's underground media, discussed above—by creating common knowledge about the alternatives the Solidarity movement offered.

The fact that the government was willing to engage opposition views on live national television illustrates the extent to which it was losing its grip on power. Recall that only a few decades earlier the communist government had had a strong hold on all forms of media and had used that power to silence opposition views instead of attempting to accommodate and incorporate them in the broader political system. At the peak of its power, the communist system did not allow for dissent or opposition, especially not in any kind of public forum.

The debate confirmed Wałęsa, both nationally and internationally, as a strong leader and serves as an example of media's power to transform opportunity for institutional change into actual institutional change. As Goban-Klas writes, "without the television opportunity, he probably could not have returned so quickly and smoothly to the Polish political scene as a popular, undisputed leader with whom the majority of Poles could identify" (1994: 201). Indeed, Wałęsa's popularity would remain intact as he was elected the President of Poland in 1990. Much to government's consternation the televised debate didn't silence the opposition movement. On the contrary Wałęsa's success led to more calls for institutional reform, contributing to a new punctuated equilibrium.

The Wałęsa–Miodowicz debate was followed by a series of "roundtable talks" beginning in February 1989, which were further meant to placate the opposition movement.[6] These talks included members of the government and key opposition leaders from the Solidarity movement. The talks, which lasted until April 1989, covered such topics as the reform of the judicial and political systems, the role of trade unions and government regulations on mass media, among others. On the political front the outcome of the roundtable talks was an agreement to changes in the political system including free elections to choose members of a new bicameral legislature and the introduction of a president to serve as chief executive. In terms of media, the outcome of the talks was a commitment to freedom of speech, allowing all political views access to the media.[7] The result was the "breakdown of the official monopoly over the media that had been a traditional feature of Communist regimes" (Goban-Klas 1994: 210). These changes marked the end of the communist rule in Poland. These punctuated institutional changes constituted a fundamental shift in Poland's economic, political, and social institutions.

A flurry of changes in the Polish media followed the roundtable talks. The changes began in June 1989 when the first elections under the new system were held. The elections could not be considered completely free since the communists implemented restrictions to maintain their position of power. Specifically, Solidarity candidates were only able to run for one-third of the seats in the lower chamber of parliament. Ultimately the Solidarity candidates won all the seats they were able to run for. Following the elections a simple system of registering newspapers and other periodicals replaced the old system. This significantly lowered the cost of starting new papers. Within months of the new registration system being established, over two thousand applications were filed. New papers emerged meeting various niche demands for a wide array of information including traditional political coverage, "light periodicals" providing entertainment and sensationalism, shopping magazines, and erotica (Goban-Klas 1997: 25).

In 1990 the law on censorship was officially revoked and legislation was introduced to begin privatizing key aspects of media infrastructure. For example, RSW *Prasa-Ksaizka-Ruch*, which had been a state-controlled organization for printing and distributing daily and weekly papers, was privatized. This was critical because it dismantled the central means of government control of the press and reallocated the infrastructure to private owners. As such the privatization created a clean break from political control and manipulation.

In our discussion of Russia we highlighted the role that political connections played in the privatization process and how those connections ultimately resulted in the failure to separate the media from the political system. The end result was the undermining of the broader transition process. The privatization of media and media infrastructure in Poland did not suffer a similar fate. The privatization process was open to both domestic and foreign parties and media outlets ended up in the hands of a wide variety of private owners. This is not to say that political connections and influences were completely absent. For example, in an effort to establish a pluralistic media, the government sold the weekly *Razem* to the Confederation of Independent Poland for a price well below book value (Gobin-Klas 1994: 223). Similar direct sales below book value took place with other media outlets as well. However, these direct sales to handpicked parties never became a binding constraint on the broader transition as they did in the case of Russia. This is because the privatization of media was considerably more open and not concentrated in the hands of a few politically connected individuals, as it was in Russia.

As another example of this latter point, consider the privatization of *Rzeczpospolita*. Under the communist regime, it was state owned and part of the government propaganda system. After the introduction of the reforms and changes discussed above, it was privatized and changed into a limited liability company. The paper was cut off from government funding and forced to survive on its own in the open marketplace. This was especially difficult in the early 1990s when Poland, like many other transition countries, faced an economic downturn. Similar to the response of media outlets to the early 1980s economic crisis in Mexico discussed above, *Rzeczpospolita* secured foreign investment from Hersant, a French newspaper group to survive. This foreign investment allowed the paper to upgrade its technology and printing plants. The journalists and employees at *Rzeczpospolita* also secured private advertising contracts, invested in training, and focused on marketing the paper as a fact-based quality paper. The approach of removing *Rzeczpospolita* from government support fostered its independence by forcing the staff to be innovative in finding the means for continued survival. This allowed the media to reinforce Poland's new punctuated equilibrium and prevented a subsequent divergence between private and public preferences.

Having established itself as a credible news source, *Rzeczpospolita* played a key role both in reinforcing the punctuated equilibrium and as a coordination-enhancing mechanism to overcome the Reformers' Dilemma. For example, it expanded its economic and political coverage and created the "green pages," which focused specifically on Poland's economic development in terms of new policies adopted, as well as their progress. The paper served as a key information source during the mass privatization efforts—and continues to provide key information on current events—allowing readers to realize the benefits and track the progress of economic reforms (Carrington and Nelson 2002: 235). Further, the addition of increased business coverage led to increased advertising revenues as advertisers sought to reach the same target market as the paper.

Expanded freedoms for broadcasting were slightly slower compared to reforms in the print media. In December 1992 the parliament passed the Broadcasting Act, which established the foundation for the operation of private commercial radio stations. The act included the rules and guidelines for operating private stations. For example, station licenses were limited to Polish citizens and stations with foreign owners who hold less than 33 per cent of the stock or capital of the company. The Broadcasting Act also established a National Broadcasting Council—*Krajowa Rada Radiofonii i Telewizji*—to oversee the licensing process and ensure that standards are met and maintained in the broadcasting industry (Naumann 2004).

Yet another significant change between the pre- and post-communist periods was the introduction of new technologies allowing media outlets to generate their product at lower costs. Specifically, many media outlets started using computers in the early 1990s not only to write stories and editorials but also to format and produce papers. As with *Rzeczpospolita*, foreign investment was a central factor behind the ability of domestic media outlets to update their technology. Indeed, by the mid-1990s the rate of foreign ownership of Polish daily newspapers was over 55 per cent. These dailies account for 70 per cent of total circulation at the national level (Goban-Klas 1997: 27; Gulyas 1999: 69, 2003: 89, 97). These technological advances further contributed to media's ability to reinforce the punctuated equilibrium by ensuring that it remained outside government control.

In January 2001 the Act on Access to Public Information was implemented. This act allows any individual the right to access public information except in those cases when the information is deemed secret by law. Further, government agencies are required to provide reports regarding their staff, budget and programs. When information requests are rejected there is a process for appealing through the court system. To date the reaction by journalists to the information law has been mixed, as there have been numerous cases of government authorities using exceptions to withhold information (Open Society Institute 2002: 447–448). Nonetheless the law does provide some foundation for information transparency, which is important for media to solve the Reformers' Dilemma by serving as a check on government.

The Impact of Media on Poland's Policies and Institutions

The media has had an important impact on several aspects of Poland's policies and institutions. The communist government used the media as a tool for coordinating Polish citizens around communist policies and ideology. The central role that media played in the communist system as a tool of propaganda illustrates media's power as a mechanism for reinforcing the existing institutional equilibrium. Indeed, the reason that the communist government invested so heavily in controlling the media was to prevent movements away from the status quo to maintain its hold on power.

The media also played a central role in the gradual erosion and eventual collapse of the communist regime, resulting in a new punctuated equilibrium. A robust underground print media developed following the emergence of the Solidarity movement in the late 1970s and was an important part of dissident efforts. This underground media served as a source of information and also as a mechanism for coordinating the actions of the Solidarity movement. Underground publications allowed Polish citizens to become aware of the presence and activities of Solidarity and provided citizens with an opportunity to update their belief systems regarding alternatives to the communist state. As an independent publisher noted,

> [A] whole network of independent publications was created, a readers' market, and a distribution system for works of literature, journalism, and academic works unhampered by censorship. These uncensored publications were only a

part, but the most important part, of a general self-defense of society against the totalitarian state apparatus (quoted in Goban-Klas 1994: 157).

The underground media facilitated gradual change by contributing to the preference gap between citizens' private preference for change and the status quo. The divergence between private and public preferences eventually led to a potential tipping point.

The media further contributed to the erosion of the communist regime through the televised Wałęsa–Miodowicz debate. The debate established Wałęsa's popularity as a capable and confident leader; it was a major event throughout the country and created common knowledge around Wałęsa's vision, as well as his role as the undisputed leader of an alternative to the communist past. In doing so media activated the tipping point created by the large preference gap that had evolved over several decades by creating common knowledge regarding the Solidarity alternative.

The Wałęsa–Miodowicz debate provides yet another example of why totalitarian regimes expend significant resources attempting to control media and information, especially regarding dissenting views and opinions. The expression of alternative views, especially when they become common knowledge as in the case of the televised debate, allows citizens to update their belief systems in ways that can weaken the control of those in power. While the goal of the Polish government in sponsoring the Wałęsa–Miodowicz debate was to placate the dissident movement, it had the opposite effect. Instead of quieting the opposition, Wałęsa's performance during the debate led to stronger demands for reforms and changes by allowing the activation of the institutional tipping point. The end result was a new punctuated equilibrium resulting in wholesale changes in economic, political, and social institutions.

As Poland's media gained independence in the early 1990s, it played an increasingly important role in the broader reform process by reinforcing the new punctuated equilibrium. The variety of independent media outlets that emerged covered the reform process and served as the main source of information for many Polish citizens, as the example of *Rzeczpospolita* illustrates. In terms of our framework, the independent media facilitated a solution to the Reformers' Dilemma by monitoring the actions of reformers and communicating that information to consumers. In this role, media reinforced reforms while further contributing to subsequent gradual changes.

Once in motion the reform process was self-extending, as citizens demanded increasing amounts of information regarding the reform process. In analyzing the success of Poland's transition relative to other transition countries, John Jackson, Jacek Klich, and Krystyna Poznanska

(2005) advance the thesis that Poland's success was grounded in the development of an extensive private sector consisting of newly founded firms. Following the failure of market socialism in the 1980s, they argue, the Polish government pursued market-based policies in the 1990s to correct for widespread market distortions, high inflation, and high foreign debt. These new policies created space for private entrepreneurship and the emergence of newly formed private firms. The initial economic reforms also created an environment conducive to foreign investment, which further spurred the development of new private firms. The emergence of the private sector put pressure on previously state-run firms, which were forced to either quickly adjust or go out of business.

Most important for our purposes is that the growth of the private sector created a class of citizens who were highly interested in the reform process. These business owners and managers had a direct interest in the implementation of liberal reforms because such reforms directly influenced their businesses. This not only reinforced existing reforms but also pressured politicians to adopt subsequent ones. Media played a key role in monitoring reformers by satisfying these consumers' demands for information regarding the reform process. Returning again to our framework, the media not only served to solve the Reformers' Dilemma but also coordinated citizens around "good conjectures." Once that equilibrium was achieved, it was self-sustaining.

Poland's media has also been an effective check on potential abuses and corruption on the part of political actors. Consider, for example, the case of Jerzy Jaskiernia. He was a key member of the SLD (Democratic Left Alliance) party and was the leader of the party's parliamentary caucus. The two most popular dailies in Poland, *Gazeta Wyborcza* and *Rzeczpospolita*, ran a series of articles investigating claims of money laundering and corruption in the gambling industry. The investigation surrounding Jaskiernia, who had been a longtime supporter of liberalization of the gambling industry, dealt with a reported $10 million bribe he accepted for his support on this issue. No official charges were brought because of a lack of evidence. But this illustrates the effectiveness of media in checking even potential corruption (Jasiewicz and Jasiewicz-Betkiewicz 2004: 1114).

As yet another example, consider the "Rywin Affair," which occurred in 2002. The chain of events associated with this corruption scandal is as follows. In July 2002 Lew Rywin, a well-known Polish film producer, approached Agora SA, the parent company of Poland's largest daily, *Gazeta Wyborcza*, presenting himself as a representative of the "group in power." In exchange for a $17.5 million payment, Rywin claimed that the group in power could make changes to a draft law dealing with the print media's influence on radio and television. The change would have worked in Agora's favor, as the current draft of the law prevented the company from becoming the owner of a private television station (Polsat) it was looking to acquire. As part of the deal Rywin asked to be appointed as the head of Agora's television network and also asked that the *Gazeta Wyborcza* refrain from criticizing the government.

Adam Michnik, the editor-in-chief at *Gazeta Wyborcza* who spoke with Rywin, secretly recorded the conversations and sought to identify the anonymous "group in power" Rywin referred to. The *Gazeta Wyborcza* eventually published part of the transcript of the Michnik–Rywin conversation, which brought the scandal to the attention of the public. In 2003 the Polish parliament formed a special committee to investigate the matter. They interviewed numerous individuals including Michnik, Rywin, Prime Minister Leszek Miller, and several other top state officials. The investigation was unable to determine with certainty who the members of the anonymous "group in power" were, though it is suspected that the group consisted of key members of the government, so no formal charges were brought against Miller or any other political leader. Rywin was prosecuted for bribery and fraud and sentenced to two years in prison and had to pay a fine (Jasiewicz and Jasiewicz-Betkiewicz 2004: 1112).

Although the members of the anonymous group were never identified, this case shows the power of media in revealing cases of corruption to the public. These are but two instances of media serving as a check on suspect behavior and corruption. There are numerous other cases where the media has played a similar role (see for instance Jasiewicz and Jasiewicz-Betkiewicz 2004: 1112–1115 and Open Society Institute 2002: 426–427). Along these lines, Jasiewicz and Jasiewicz-Betkiewicz note that,

> The role played in this field [identifying corruption] by the media—central as much as local, print as much as broadcast—constitutes the sunny side of Poland's young democracy. The press, even if oftentimes short on professionalism, is truly devoted to its role as the fourth estate (2004: 1114).

Media freedom has been institutionalized in Poland. The 1997 constitution forbids censorship and guarantees freedom of the press. Both have been enforced since the fall of communism. A large majority of the press remains privately owned although the state does own and operate several television stations (for example, TVP 1, TVP 2 and TVP Polonia) and radio stations (for example, Program 1 and Program 2). For the most part journalists and media employees operate in an environment free from coercion. One current concern is the presence of insult laws that can be used to punish journalists. There is some concern that the use of these laws may increase or lead to self-censorship (Freedom House 2007). Despite these concerns, Poland's media operates in an environment generally free from government manipulation.

Summation

The case of Poland offers several important lessons in the context of our analysis. First, Poland again illustrates how even a relatively unfree media can contribute to the process of policy and institutional change. Although limited in its reach because of legal constraints, the underground media played a key role in generating a wedge between private and public preferences. The resulting tipping point was activated by the televised debate which created common knowledge around alternative perceptions and ideas. The end result was a new punctuated equilibrium.

Another key lesson is that deregulation of the media should take place as early in the reform process as possible. In Poland media freedom was part of the initial reforms demanded by the Solidarity movement in their conversations with the communist government. Media deregulation was also discussed during the roundtable talks in 1989 and a number of immediate media reforms were implemented following the end of the talks. These reforms included simplifying the registration process, removing mechanisms of government censorship, and beginning the process of privatizing state-owned media outlets and infrastructure. The faster the media is freed from regulation, the faster it can develop as an independent entity and a solution to the Reformers' Dilemma.

A related lesson is that media should be separated from the political apparatus as quickly as possible. This includes not only privatizing state-owned media but also removing all government subsidies and financing, as well as any price controls on media product or inputs used to produce media products. In the case of Russia, failure to separate the media from the political system resulted in the undermining of the broader reform process. In Poland, in contrast, privatized media outlets were forced to be entrepreneurial in finding ways to be financially sustainable absent government support. This allowed a truly independent media to emerge.

The case of Poland also highlights the importance of foreign investment in the development of an independent press. As the example of *Rzeczpospolita* illustrates, foreign investors can be an important source of financing for privatized media outlets. In the case of Poland, Millard notes that "foreign firms set up publishing houses, established journals modeled on successes elsewhere, and purchased existing publications, sometimes with Polish partners" (2004: 90). In general, opening the media industry to foreign owners and investors fosters media independence because foreigners are typically not subject to the same political pressures as domestic owners. As discussed throughout this book, foreign influence is not just important in terms of financing but also in terms of the exchange of journalistic standards and media management practices and techniques.

Finally, Poland illustrates the importance of creating a general environment conducive to private entrepreneurship. A free media by itself does not guarantee successful outcomes in terms of development. Consumers must demand certain information and policies from reformers. In Poland the emergence of a robust private sector consisting of new firms created a demand for subsequent reforms and information associated with those reforms. This demand, coupled with the early reforms to create an independent media, allowed the media to serve as a solution to the Reformers' Dilemma. In this role media was able to reinforce existing reforms while simultaneously contributing to the adoption of subsequent reforms. Once the Reformers' Dilemma was solved and Polish citizens coordinated around good conjectures, the equilibrium was self-sustaining and self-extending.

NOTES

1. From 1994 through 2001, the channel was known as ORT, after which it was renamed Channel One.
2. Berezovsky's holding company included ORT, TV6 and the newspapers *Nezavisimaya Gazeta*, *Novye Izvestiya* and *Kommersant*.
3. Channel Russia has been state owned since its founding in 1991. As we discussed earlier in this chapter, ORT and NTV were owned by private individuals before they sold their shares to individuals, or groups of individuals, loyal to the Kremlin.
4. For a discussion of alternative methods of privatization, see Anderson (2004: 91–92).
5. The Polish government in power prior to the Soviet and Russian invasions fled to London to form a government in exile. This was led by Prime Minister Władysław Sikorski, and was recognized by the Allied governments as the legal and rightful government of Poland.
6. On the expectations and miscalculations of the communist government regarding the roundtable talks, see Hayden (2001).
7. For a detailed account of the roundtable discussion on media, see Goban-Klas (1990).

REFERENCES

Anderson, Robert E. (2004) *Just Get Out of the Way: How Government Can Help Business in Poor Countries*. Washington, DC: Cato Institute.

Androunas, Elana (1993) *Soviet Media Transition: Structural and Economic Alternatives*. Westport, CT: Praeger.

Baker, Peter (2005) "In Russian Media, Free Speech for a Select Few," *The Washington Post*, 25 February: A18.

Becker, Jonathan (2002) *Soviet and Russian Press Coverage of the United States*. London: Palgrave.

Becker, Jonathan (2004) "Lessons from Russia: A Neo-Authoritarian Media System," *European Journal of Communication*, 19(2): 139–163.

Belin, Laura (2001) "Bias and Self-Censorship in the Media." In Archie Brown (ed.), *Contemporary Russian Politics*. Oxford: Oxford University Press, pp. 323–344.

Benn, David Wedgwood (1996) "The Russian Media in Post-Soviet Conditions," *Europe-Asia Studies*, 48(3): 471–479.

Boettke, Peter J. (1993) *Why Perestroika Failed: The Politics and Economics of Socialist Transformation*. New York: Routledge.

Bożyk, Pawel (2006) *Globalization and the Transformation of Foreign Economic Policy*. Burlington, VT: Ashgate Publishing Ltd.

Carrington, Tim and Mark Nelson (2002) 'Media in Transition: The Hegemony of Economics'. In Alisa Clapp-Itnyre, Roumeen Islam and Caralee McLiesh (eds), *The Right to Tell: The Role of Mass Media in Economic Development*. Washington, DC: The World Bank, pp. 225–248.

Dowing, John D.H. (1996) *Internationalizing Media Theory: Transition, Power and Culture*. London: Sage Publications.

Freedom House (2007) *Freedom of the Press 2007: A Global Survey of Media Independence*. New York: Rowinon and Littlefield.

Goban-Klas, Tomasz (1990) "Making Media Policy in Poland," *Journal of Communication*, 40(1): 50–54.

Goban-Klas, Tomasz (1994) *The Orchestration of the Media: The Politics of Mass Communications in Communist Poland and the Aftermath*. Boulder, CO: Westview Press.

Goban-Klas, Tomasz (1997) "Politics versus the Media in Poland: A Game without Rules." In Patrick H.O'Neil (ed.), *Post-Communism and the Media in Eastern Europe*. London: Frank Cass, pp. 24–41.

Gulyas, Agnes (1999) "Structural Changes and Organizations in the Print Media Markets of Post Communist East Central Europe," *The Public*, 6(2): 61–74.

Gulyas, Agnes (2003) "Print Media in Post-Communist East Central Europe," *European Journal of Communication*, 18(1): 81–106.

Hayden, Jacqueline (2001) "Explaining the Collapse of Communism in Poland: Strategic Misperceptions and Unanticipated Outcomes," *The Journal of Communist Studies and Transition Politics*, 17(4): 108–129.

Hollander, Gayle D. (1972) *Soviet Political Indoctrination: Developments in Mass Media and Propaganda Since Stalin*. New York: Praeger Publishers.

Hopkins, Mark (1970) *Mass Media in the Soviet Union*. New York: Western Publishing Companies.

Hughes, Sallie (2006) *Newsrooms in Conflict: Journalism and the Democratization of Mexico*. Pittsburgh, PA: University of Pittsburgh Press.

Jackson, John E., Jacek Klich and Krystyna Poznanska (2005) *The Political Economy of Poland's Transition: New Firms and Reform Governments*. Cambridge: Cambridge University Press.

Jasiewicz, Krzysztof and Agnieszka Jasiewicz-Betkiewicz (2004) "Poland," *European Journal of Political Research*, 43: 1106–1115.

Lawson, Chappell H. (2002) *Building the Fourth Estate: Democratization and the Rise of a Free Press in Mexico*. Berkeley, CA: University of California Press.

Leeson, Peter T. and William N. Trumbull (2006) "Comparing Apples: Normalcy, Russia, and the Remaining Post-Socialist World," *Post-Soviet Affairs*, 22(3): 225–248.

Lipman, Masha and Michael McFaul (2001) "Managed Democracy in Russia: Putin and the Press," *Harvard Journal of Press/Politics*, 6(3): 116–126.

Mickiewicz, Ellen (2000) "Institutional Incapacity, the Attentive Public, and Media Pluralism in Russia." In Gunther, Richard and Mughan, Anthony (eds), *Democracy and the Media*, Cambridge: Cambridge University Press, pp. 85–121.

Millard, Frances (1998) "Democratization and Media in Poland." In Vicky Randall (ed.), *Democratization and the Media*. New York: Routledge, pp. 85–105.

Naumann, Jerzy (2004) *Media System in Poland*. Hamburg: Hans-Bredow Institut.

Open Society Institute (2002) *Monitoring the EU Accession Process: Corruption and Anti-corruption Policy*. Budapest: EU Monitoring and Advocacy Program of the Open Society Institute.

Petro, Nicolai N. (2007) "Russia as friend, not foe," *Asia Times Online*, 17 February. http://www.atimes.com/atimes/Central_Asia/IB17Ag02.html, accessed 11 January 2009.

Reporters Sans Frontières (2007) *Press Freedom in 2007*. Paris: Reporters Sans Frontières.

Sparks, Colin (2000) "Media Theory after the Fall of Communism." In James Curran and Myung-Jin Park (eds), *De-Westernizing Media Studies*. New York: Routledge, pp. 35–49.

Sparks, Colin (1998) "Media Systems in Transition: Poland, Russia, China," *Chinese Journal of Communication*, 1: 7–24.

Turpin, Jennifer (1995) *Reinventing the Soviet Self: Media and Social Change in the Former Soviet Union*. Westport, CT: Praeger.

Vargas-Llosa, Mario (1991) "Mexico: The Perfect Dictatorship," *New Perspectives Quarterly*, 8(1): 23–24.

Zassoursky, Ivan (2004) *Media and Power in Post-Soviet Russia*. New York: M.E. Sharpe.

6. Conclusion—implications for policy

INTRODUCTION

In this book we have analyzed the role of media in economic development and institutional change. We considered the important role of media as a check on the behavior of government. We also discussed how media can serve as a solution to the Reformers' Dilemma and considered the wide array of factors influencing media's effectiveness in this regard. Media can influence policies within given institutions while simultaneously serving as a mechanism of institutional change and reinforcement. We highlighted three effects of media on institutional change—the gradual effect, the punctuation effect, and the reinforcement effect. The statistical analyses and case studies explored these various aspects of media. A central theme of our analysis is that a free media is a "first-best" situation. Where media is free, it is best able to serve as a check on government while providing a solution to the Reformers' Dilemma. In reality, however, the first-best outcome of a free media is rarely achieved. Indeed, a central part of our analysis was to highlight how even a relatively unfree media can contribute to changes in policies and institutions. Nonetheless, any movement toward the first best outcome of a free media is preferable for the reasons discussed throughout this book. Given this, our study has prescriptive implications for policymakers in developing countries and those working for international organizations attempting to assist developing countries.

In this concluding chapter we identify and summarize the implications of our analysis. We first reiterate why a free media is a first best in the context of economic development. Next, we provide some clear policy steps toward increasing media freedom in developing countries. We then discuss the sequencing of media freedom and subsequent reforms. Where media is unfree, initial reforms are needed to increase media independence and to allow it to serve as a solution to the Reformers' Dilemma. We discuss how these initial reforms might emerge. Finally, we turn to a consideration of the issues associated with "market failures" in media and information markets. Our analysis suggests that the costs of correcting alleged market failures in the media industry are likely to exceed the benefits of such "correction," especially in developing nations where a free media is most important. On this basis we argue that governments in developing countries should not intervene to correct perceived market failures in media markets.

WHY A FREE MEDIA?

We identified two main reasons why a free media is a first-best situation for economic development. The first is that a free media serves as a check on political actors. As Amartya Sen (1984, 1999) has emphasized, a free media, coupled with political competition, pressures political actors to adopt policies that go beyond their own narrow interests. The underlying logic is that failure by those in power to act in the public's interest will lead to a political backlash. To the extent that media is effective in this role, there will be pressure on officials to respond to citizens' demands. As the cases of Russia and Poland illustrate, even where media is unfree, unofficial media may persist, creating some degree of media freedom despite government's attempts to suppress it. Similarly, political competition exists to some extent even where government is dictatorial. Although a free media under democracy maximizes media's ability to constrain political actors and facilitate development-enhancing change, media can still play some role even where these first-best conditions are not satisfied.

While research in the area of media and economic development has analyzed how media can serve as a check on government, this research has not provided a complete understanding of how media can provide the incentive for officials to adopt policies that are conducive to economic development. To fill this gap we developed the Reformers' Dilemma model (see Chapter 2) to capture the fundamental problem facing developing countries. As the model indicates, absent a coordination-enhancing mechanism, political agents with the power to implement reforms will typically lack the incentive to do so. Instead of adopting reforms that have far-reaching benefits for the citizens of the developing country, political actors will tend to pursue their own narrow interests by catering to special-interest groups. The result will be continued economic stagnation and failure to reform. A free media, by creating an effective monitoring device and supplying citizens with the means to punish defecting politicians, can overcome the Reformers' Dilemma by coordinating reformers on the cooperative outcome of adopting beneficial reforms.

The second reason a free media is important for economic development is that it facilitates policy and institutional change. As Chapter 1 discussed, the process of institutional change typically involves gradual changes in the belief systems of members of a society. This process leads to marginal changes in existing institutions. It is also possible for media to generate dramatic changes in institutional arrangements, leading to new punctuated institutional equilibria. This involves fundamental changes in the very nature of institutions. Finally, media can have a reinforcement effect whereby it coordinates citizens and policymakers on new punctuated equilibria.

Given its ability to reach large numbers of consumers and create common knowledge around new perceptions and ideas, we argued that the media is one important mechanism for facilitating gradual and dramatic institutional change, as well as for reinforcing changes once they occur. Within the Reformers' Dilemma framework, the process of institutional change is captured by the coordination game in Chapter 2 (Figure 2.3). The process of institutional change requires widespread coordination on new conjectures and economic development requires coordination specifically on "good" conjectures. We argued that the speed of these changes will be a function of citizen preferences for change, as well as the "preference gap" between citizens' preferences and their ability to publicly voice those preferences.

As we have emphasized, a free media is a necessary but not sufficient condition for economic development and institutional change. Consumer demand for certain types of information and certain types of reforms are required for a free media to be effective in solving the Reformers' Dilemma. If consumers are either uninterested in reforms, or demand reforms that fail to support economic development, a free media will be ineffective in providing a solution to the Reformers' Dilemma. While these factors are largely exogenous to media freedom, they are also at least partly endogenous in that, as we discussed in Chapter 4, the level of media independence in a country can contribute to citizens' political interest or apathy.

POLICY IMPLICATIONS

Given the first best of a free and independent media, our analysis yields specific implications for policymakers. These policy recommendations constitute a list of "best practices" regarding media in developing countries, with full recognition that any movement toward the ideal of a free media is preferable to the status quo. In most cases, immediate movement toward adopting each reform fully will not be feasible given political constraints. However, as the case of Poland illustrates, it is possible for large-scale media reforms to be adopted in a relatively short time.

1. Privatize all Aspects of Media as Quickly as Possible

Media outlets, as well as the infrastructure used to produce media products, should be removed from government control as quickly as possible and transferred to private owners. For an independent media to emerge, the media apparatus must be separated from the political system. The separation of the media and political system goes beyond direct control—state ownership and management—to include also indirect forms of government control—government subsidies, favorable tax treatment, entry regulation, and so on. As discussed in Chapter 3, indirect forms of government manipulation prevent the emergence of an independent media and can undermine the broader reform process.

Failure in this regard can also have a negative effect on media's credibility in consumers' eyes. When the information provided by media is viewed as inaccurate or incomplete, consumers find it more difficult to effectively monitor the actions of politicians. In such circumstances, the media is less likely to solve the Reformers' Dilemma. The credibility crisis can also lead to a growing preference gap between true private preferences and publicly revealed preferences. When this occurs, dramatic institutional change is more likely, resulting in greater instability of existing institutional arrangements.

As our analysis of government manipulation of media in Chapter 3 discussed, indirect manipulation of media is just as important as direct manipulation. For this reason, media must not only be removed from direct government control through privatization, but also from indirect forms of manipulation that exist despite nominal private ownership of media outlets. Ideally, this entails removing *all* indirect forms of government manipulation, including financial subsidies and loans, tax breaks and debt forgiveness. It also entails removing ambiguous regulations (for example, licensing, registration, tax codes, and building codes) that can be used to manipulate the media. Such regulations refer not only to those that apply specifically to the media industry, but also to those that apply more generally to a country's comprehensive business climate. Where regulations are numerous, ambiguous, or change frequently, those in positions of power can use regulatory infractions to constrain media outlets that refuse to engage in favorable reporting.

As the case of Poland suggests, separating the media from the political apparatus should occur as quickly as possible (see Chapter 5). Recall that in Poland, media was not only privatized, but also separated from government financial support in a relatively short time. This forced media outlets to develop strategies for remaining financially independent and allowed the media to develop as an independent entity. In stark contrast, the Russian media remained closely connected to the political system and failed to develop as an independent entity. In the absence of an effective solution to the Reformers' Dilemma, the broader reform process was undermined.

Efforts to create an independent media should not be phased in over time, but rather should be implemented as quickly as possible. Reforms that attempt to gradually create an independent media will only slow the process and increase the probability of political obstruction. Perhaps the fastest way to develop an independent media is to legalize all underground media publications. By definition, underground media outlets have developed without state support or interference. As such, these publications are already independent and self-sustaining. As the cases of Poland and Russia indicate, a robust underground media can develop even where the state controls the legal media industry. Removing the constraints associated with being deemed illegal will allow these media outlets to move above ground and serve as the foundation for an independent media industry. Most importantly, it will remove the control of the media from those in positions of political power. These individuals will tend to have an interest in maintaining control over the media for their own narrow interests at the expense of the broader reform process.

As we saw in the case of Russia, economic downturns can lead to calls for government interventions in the form of subsidies, advertising contracts, and so on. Such interventions should be avoided, even in the case of economic hardship. Government support, even if motivated by benevolent concerns, opens up the possibility of government manipulation in current or future periods. Given this, direct and indirect government interventions should not be viewed as a viable alternative if an independent media is the desired goal. Any form of government support is likely to exacerbate media dependence instead of contributing to the emergence of an independent media.

2. Open, Unconditional Auctions are the Best Means of Media Privatization

Given the goal of removing media from political control as quickly as possible, the central question becomes the best means of privatization. Following Anderson (2004: 96–120), we contend that the best means of privatizing media assets is for the government to hold an open and unconditional auction in which assets are awarded to the highest cash bid. The auction should be open to both domestic and foreign bidders. Further, it should be unconditional, meaning government should not put restrictions on bidders in terms of promises of future investments or in terms of the quality of bidders or business plan.

Of course this method of privatization is far from perfect.[1] For example, it is still possible for wealthy and politically-connected individuals to bid for media outlets and potentially win the auction. However, this method is the best means of minimizing the issues associated with crony capitalism whereby state assets are pseudo-privatized and sold to individuals who are connected to the political elite. As the case of Russia illustrates, the adverse impact of crony capitalism on the emergence of an independent media is a central concern for the success of subsequent reforms. An open auction, where the asset is awarded to the highest cash bid, increases transparency and ensures that assets end up in the hands of those individuals who value them the most. Further, making auctions open to foreign investors makes it more likely that bidding will be competitive and that a pluralistic media industry will develop.

It is also important to note that formerly state-owned media assets are not the only resource for media outlets. If other steps are taken to create an environment conducive to entrepreneurship and innovation, new private media firms will also emerge to compete with and complement previously state-owned media outlets. This will further contribute to a diversified media. In this regard, a key aspect of the privatization process is removing barriers to entry, both in the media industry and related industries. Media outlets that fail to meet consumer demands must be allowed to fail and exit the market, and new media outlets must be allowed to enter the market and offer their products. Open entry and exit contributes to increased competition and prevents any one media outlet from achieving any kind of permanent monopoly through government privilege. As discussed in the case of Poland, the emergence of a sector of new private firms in a wide variety of industries contributed to the demand for increased reforms and information regarding those reforms. A similar logic applies to the media industry. An environment conducive to private investment and innovation will contribute to an independent and diverse media industry.

3. Open Borders to Foreign Ownership, Investment, and Influence

Opening the borders of developing countries to foreign investment, ownership, and media influence is a critical step in establishing an independent media for several reasons. In their empirical analysis of the media, Besley and Prat (2006) find that foreign ownership is positively correlated with media freedom and negatively correlated with government corruption. As discussed above, allowing for foreign investment creates competition among bidders for media assets and lowers the likelihood that those assets will end up in the hands of individuals who are politically connected. Further, foreign owners tend to be insulated from government attempts to manipulate the media relative to domestic media outlets, which are more likely to be subject to political pressures.

Allowing foreign ownership and investment has other important benefits. The potential for foreign investment provides a solution to financial independence for media outlets. As the case studies in the previous chapter indicated, obtaining private sources of financing can be critical for media independence, especially in the early stages following privatization. Foreign investors and owners can provide financial support that allows media outlets to develop without government support. Foreign investment not only allows media outlets to continue operations but also to update and increase their capital. This is precisely what happened in the case of Poland, where foreign investment played a central role in the creation of an independent media by allowing media outlets to sustain and evolve without government support.

Yet another area in which foreign influence can contribute to the emergence of an independent media is in the development of journalistic standards and ethics, as well as the management techniques associated with operating a media outlet. A central issue in many developing countries is the media's quality. Because it is typically underdeveloped relative to the media in developed countries, journalistic standards and ethical guidelines are often lacking. Similarly, knowledge of management techniques and organizational forms are typically absent in developing countries. Opening borders to foreign influences provides one solution to the issues associated with media quality. When foreign firms have access to the domestic market, and vice versa, journalistic standards, ethical guidelines, management techniques, and organizational forms can be imported from abroad. This allows for the emulation of existing and established media institutions.

The possibility for emulation afforded by exposure to foreign media outlets goes beyond purely media-related institutions such as journalistic standards, norms, and management techniques. In general, the exposure of domestic citizens to foreign media allows the exchange of information and ideas. In this sense, exposure to foreign media can contribute to the process of institutional change by creating common knowledge around different ideas and world views. Access to foreign media expands the menu of media products available to domestic citizens, as well as the array of information and ideas. Fear of foreign ownership and influence often leads to restrictions on foreign ownership and investment in domestic media. However, this xenophobia constrains the emergence of an independent media while overlooking the significant economic and cultural benefits of free trade.[2] Given this, laws designed to restrict foreign investment and foster cultural protection should be removed so that information and ideas are free to flow between countries.

As emphasized throughout this book, exposure to foreign media is not a guarantee of "good" policy and institutional change. Stated differently, there is no guarantee that citizens in developing countries will consume the information produced by foreign media, let alone update their belief systems accordingly. Despite the potential for this outcome, increasing the array of media products, and the diversity of information and ideas they provide, at least offers the possibility of policy and institutional change resulting in economic development, and therefore is the best strategy if economic development is the desired goal.

4. Establish and Enforce Laws Increasing Information Transparency

To be an effective solution to the Reformers' Dilemma, media outlets must have access to timely and accurate information. This is important for reporting on current events and also for verifying the past decisions and information provided by political actors. Access to accurate information is also important for establishing a reputation of credibility with consumers. In the absence of accurate and timely information, media outlets will be a less effective check on political actors and will suffer from credibility issues with the public. Information transparency also contributes to an environment of competition between media outlets. Independent media outlets will attempt to report information quickly and accurately in order to beat other media outlets to the market with relevant information. Transparency laws have the additional benefit of lowering the cost of revealing misreporting and inaccuracies because media outlets can access information to verify the reporting of other media outlets.

Reformers must establish information laws that allow for information transparency, including access to information, in a timely manner. These laws must provide clear guidelines regarding what information can be accessed, as well as guidelines for requesting information and a process of appeal if requests are delayed or rejected. While establishing an official information law is the first step, the law must be implemented and followed to be effective. Recall from our discussion in Chapter 3 that many countries have information laws on the books but suffer from problems associated with unintentional or intentional delays.

Unintentional delays refer to delays in requests for information due to ineffective or inefficient administration. These delays are purely a matter of bureaucratic inefficiencies and can be addressed by better understanding the incentives facing bureaucrats (see Mises 1944; Tullock 1965; Niskanen 1971). In contrast, intentional delays for information requests occur when government officials purposefully delay fulfilling requests to prevent the media from obtaining certain information. When government officials can abuse information laws by intentionally delaying information disclosure, it severely constrains the effectiveness of transparency laws because the media cannot report information in a timely manner. Both types of delays limit the effectiveness of information laws. The difference is the cause of each type and the resulting remedy. Remedies for unintentional delays involve recognizing the limits of bureaucratic activity and developing rules to facilitate information sharing and incentive alignment. Remedies for intentional delays entail the establishment of constraints and checks and balances on government officials to prevent abuse of transparency laws.

In order to be effective, freedom of information laws must be accompanied by a set of complementary rules and guidelines. These include an effective process for administering requests and for appealing requests that are rejected. Further, there must be clear checks on government officials to prevent them from abusing information laws by intentionally delaying the release of information. One such check would be an effective process for filing complaints regarding requests that are rejected or not filled within a specific period of time.

5. Establish and Enforce Laws Protecting Media Employees and Journalists from Coercion

It may seem obvious that journalists and media employees must be protected from physical concern (for example, physical attacks and murder) and the threat of jail for doing their job. However, as we saw in Chapter 3, the threat of coercion against journalists and media employees continues to be very real in many countries throughout the world. The policy implication here is straightforward—developing countries must take steps to protect journalists and media employees in order for an independent media to emerge. At a minimum, this involves the establishment and enforcement of basic protections of person and property that should extend to all citizens in a free society.

Indirect forms of coercion, such as insult laws, provide another problem for many journalists and media employees. Insult laws are rules that make it illegal to criticize government officials or members of the ruling elite. The goal is to abolish insult laws altogether. Attempts to rewrite or revise existing laws should be avoided because they leave open the possibility that the laws can be abused in the future. Future abuses are more likely to occur in developing countries where the checks and balances on government are relatively weak.

Following the recommendation made by Walden (2002: 216–217), criminal penalties for libel and slander should also be abolished and cases along these lines should be handled within the context of civil laws. Further, checks and standards must be established to determine guilt in slander and libel cases to prevent the overuse of these laws by political officials who are dissatisfied with the reporting of media outlets. For instance, if all that is required for guilt is allegations by government officials against journalists, we would expect slander and libel laws to be overused. The solution entails a set of checks and balances that raise the cost of erroneous charges and allegations and therefore the potential abuse of slander and libel laws.

WHICH COMES FIRST—A FREE MEDIA OR REFORMS?

A central issue within the framework and analysis developed in this book is the initial catalyst that begins the reform process toward the end goals discussed above. This issue can be summarized as follows. The policy recommendations made above will improve the media's effectiveness as a solution to the Reformers' Dilemma. However, the adoption of reforms in the media industry, just like in any other industry, may suffer from the obstacle described by the Reformers' Dilemma. Stated differently, in order to adopt reforms in the media industry, reformers must have some initial incentive despite the absence of a free media. But where is this initial incentive to come from without a free media to provide pressure?

For initial media reforms to take hold, at least a partial solution to the Reformers' Dilemma must be found. Absent some pressure on reformers, they will have no incentive to adopt initial reforms of the media so that it can develop as a subsequent solution to the Reformers' Dilemma in the context of non-media-related economic reforms. Once media independence has reached some critical threshold, its ability to solve the Reformers' Dilemma becomes institutionalized and contributes to the adoption of subsequent reforms as described in the analysis in this book. There are several "solutions" to this apparent paradox.

One potential catalyst of change is some form of exogenous shock to the broader status quo that generates a series of reforms. The case studies in the previous chapter provided several examples of this. In the case of Poland, the rise of the Solidarity movement led to a robust underground press and eventually pressured the communist government to adopt reforms, including those in the media sector. In Mexico, an economic crisis led to reforms that created space for the media to gain increasing independence. As these examples indicate, the initial emergence of media freedom is often the result of some exogenous shock to the broader political, economic, and social system. Further, once the reform process is in motion, reforms can be self-sustaining and self-extending. For example, as discussed in the case of Poland, the initial reforms led to a series of subsequent reforms both in the media industry and in other industries.

This recognition of exogenous shocks is simply the recognition that the media does not exist in a vacuum. Instead, it is influenced and constrained by economic, political, and social institutions. As those institutions change—due to a variety of potential factors—there will be changes in the media industry. When an opportunity for change arises due to exogenous factors, the media can play a key role in being a catalyst of change and then reinforcement.

In addition to exogenous shocks, another catalyst of change is alternative sources of information that pressure reformers to take initial steps toward increased media independence. Examples include information provided by think tanks, government and media watchdog groups, academics, and political campaigns, which can also serve to monitor political agents. Where media independence does not yet exist, these alternative sources of information can provide partial solutions to the Reformers' Dilemma, which can begin the process of reform and change.

Finally, even where the broader media is largely unfree, certain aspects of it can still serve as a catalyst of change. As discussed in the previous chapter, a robust underground media developed in both Poland and Russia, providing alternative views and information. This led to an increasing preference gap between the desire for change on the part of citizens and what was publicly revealed due to government control. When external factors created the conditions for change, the underground media played a key role in serving as a catalyst of change, ultimately resulting in new punctuated equilibria. Once this occurred, the media was able to coordinate citizens on subsequent reforms and change.

MARKET FAILURE IN MEDIA MARKETS

A central issue addressed in the media economics literature is the possibility that unregulated media and information markets may fail (see for instance Brown 1996; Ludwig 2000; Baker 2002; Hoskins, McFadyen and Finn 2004: 287–303). A "market failure" is said to occur when an unregulated market does not achieve allocative efficiency. Allocative efficiency exists when resources are allocated to the production of goods and services such that the benefit to society of the last unit produced is equal to the cost to society of producing that last unit. The potential for market failures is a standard justification for government intervention in markets. In theory, where market failures exist, the government can intervene to reallocate resources toward the ideal end of allocative efficiency. Three main market failures—externalities, public goods, and lack of competition—are commonly cited in the context of media markets.

Given the importance of these issues for the effective operation of the media industry, it is important for us to consider these arguments in the context of our call for a first-best situation where media is free from government control and intervention. In this section we review the standard arguments on market failures in the media industry. In the next section we discuss why market failure arguments should not be used as justification for government intervention in media markets in developing countries in particular.

The first market failure deals with the externality aspects of information. An externality exists when an action yields costs (a negative externality) or benefits (a positive externality) that accrue to individuals not involved in the actual act. The standard example of a negative externality is pollution. This produces a spillover cost to individuals not directly involved in the production of the pollution. An example of a positive externality is scientific research where those not directly involved in the production of the research receive a spillover benefit from others' work. In theory, negative externalities are oversupplied on the unregulated market and positive externalities are undersupplied.

Writers applying the logic of externalities to media markets reach conclusions along the following lines:

> They [media markets] provide too much 'bad' quality content – bad meaning content that has negative externalities. Media markets also may produce a wasteful abundance of content responding to mainstream tastes. Otherwise, the main problem is underproduction. Markets predictably provide inadequate amounts and inadequate diversity of media content – quality meaning content that has positive externalities (Baker 2002: 96–97).

In response to externality arguments, the standard policy implication is that government should intervene to reduce the amount of media-generated negative externalities, while increasing the amount of media-produced positive externalities. In practice, governments throughout the world have typically used some combination of subsidies, content rules, and direct state ownership to achieve these ends. Government subsidies to media outlets vary in their allocation and magnitude, but governments have given subsidies to television stations, radio stations, and newspapers. Content rules typically dictate what can be covered by media outlets, as well as the proportion of coverage. Examples may include requirements on the number of hours for children's programming, documentaries, and government programming, and the nature and content of programs shown (for example, levels of violence, or language) (Baker 2002: 98–114; Hoskins, McFadyen and Finn 2004: 293–295).

A second and related market failure deals with the "public good" aspects of the media. A public good has two specific characteristics. The first is that it is non-rivalrous, meaning that one individual's consumption does not reduce others' ability to consume the good. The second characteristic is that it is non-excludable, which means that once the good is produced, individuals cannot be prevented from consuming it. Basic television programs available to all those who own a television set are an example of a public good. Basic television is non-rivalrous in that one person's consumption of a television show does not reduce others' ability to consume the same show. Likewise, once a television show is airing, it is non-excludable because anyone with a television set can consume the program. In theory, public goods are undersupplied on the unregulated market because of issues associated with free riding and pricing.[3]

The standard solution to problems associated with public goods is for government to directly provide the good in question. In the media market, government ownership and operation of public broadcasting stations (for example, the BBC and the Australian Broadcasting Corporation) is one example of this logic. Yet another solution, similar to the case of positive externalities, is for government to subsidize the production of the under-supplied media product to make up for the shortfall.

The market structure of the media industry is yet another source of potential market failure. In theory, the presence of a monopoly producer will result in the failure to achieve allocative efficiency. Monopolists underproduce the good in question and charge a higher price when compared to perfectly competitive firms. Monopolies can arise through government privilege (for example, entry regulation, licensing) or through a process whereby a single producer of a good or service emerges due to the costs associated with production. This latter case describes a "natural monopoly" and arises when significant economies of scale result in a single provider. When a natural monopoly exists, a single producer can serve the entire market at a lower average cost than multiple competitive firms. Because of the large fixed costs associated with establishing the required infrastructure, it has been argued that telephone and cable providers, as well as Internet companies, constitute natural monopolies.

There are several forms of government intervention aimed at correcting for inefficiencies associated with monopolies in the media industry. One is government assuming direct control of media outlets. The underlying logic behind this intervention is that government can produce more output and charge a lower price compared to a private monopoly. Another common response, especially in the case of natural monopoly, is government regulation. Government regulates the rates many telecommunications and cable companies charge. These regulations typically cover output, price, and product characteristics. Similar to the previously discussed interventions, these regulations attempt to overcome market failures by ensuring allocative efficiency in the media market.

WHY GOVERNMENTS IN DEVELOPING COUNTRIES SHOULD *NOT* INTERVENE IN MEDIA MARKETS

At first blush, the potential for market failures in the media industry provides justification for government interventions in media markets. In contrast to this view, we contend that governments should refrain from intervening in media markets to correct for perceived market failures, especially in developing countries. There are a number of reasons to be skeptical of government's ability to effectively intervene in this market. These problems are magnified in developing countries where checks and balances on governments are weak or non-existent.

One reason to be skeptical of government intervention in the media industry is that government agents suffer from a fundamental knowledge problem. Recall that market failures emerge from the inability of unregulated markets to achieve allocative efficiency. In theory, government interventions can contribute to the achievement of this ideal. However, this justification for government intervention in the market assumes that government agents know the "optimal" level of output and price necessary to achieve allocative efficiency in media markets. There is no reason to believe that political actors have special access to this information, which as F.A. Hayek (1945) pointed out, is in fact only generated through the market process in the first place.

When the government intervenes in the media market, the issue becomes how much media to supply, to whom, and at what price. These are the same questions that face private media firms. The issue for private media is not whether to provide media products per se, but what types of media products to produce and how much of each type to produce. The difference between private firms and the government is that the former acts in the context of prices, profits, and losses, while the latter does not. This context allows private firms to engage in rational economic calculation to determine the types of media product to provide, as well as the level of output and the appropriate price.[4] Governments act outside the context of prices and profit and loss, and therefore have no means of engaging in economic calculation and hence no way of knowing how to effectively allocate resources. Given the calculation constraint facing government actors, there is good reason for skepticism regarding their ability to achieve allocative efficiency.

Government regulations and subsidies, which allow for private ownership and production but attempt to intervene in how private firms allocate resources, fail to solve the problems just discussed. Regulations of price, output level, and product characteristics assume that government officials know the "right" levels of output, the "right" price and the "right" characteristics of the products. However, in the absence of any criteria for engaging in economic calculation, government officials will be left to guess the correct level of output or the correct price. Even if officials know that a particular media product is undersupplied on the market and therefore that more should be produced, there is no reason to think that they will produce the correct amount. In attempting to correct the undersupply they may in fact create an oversupply as large, or larger, in magnitude than the market underprovision. This is a serious problem since, from an efficiency standpoint, one "unit" of oversupply is as inefficient as one "unit" of undersupply.

Along similar lines, the payment of subsidies to media producers assumes that government knows how to allocate those funds to generate allocative efficiency. When a government subsidizes a specific type of media product, it will clearly generate more of that product than existed prior to the subsidy. But how will government officials know the level of the subsidy or to whom to give the subsidy? While the overall level of output will increase, it is far from clear that the ultimate outcome will resemble any notion of allocative efficiency. Further, in the absence of the profit and loss mechanism, government officials will have no means of feedback. In other words, they will have no means of knowing if they have allocated resources correctly or incorrectly, whether they have achieved allocative efficiency, or whether they have overshot and produced too much of the good in question.

The second argument against government interventions in the media market as a remedy for perceived market failures follows from the knowledge problem just discussed. In the absence of criteria for engaging in economic calculation, various political pressures will be the main factor guiding the magnitude and extent of government interventions. The nature of these pressures will vary depending on the nature of the political system. However, as the many examples and case studies throughout this book have indicated, political leaders tend to act in their self-interest rather than pursuing some notion of the public interest. Thus, alongside the knowledge problem that government confronts in attempting to remedy market failures in the media industry, there is also a significant incentive problem.

For example, in the case studies in the previous chapter we noted that political officials invested significant resources in controlling the nature and content of the media to maintain their positions of power. We also saw the role that political pressures played in media's privatization in Russia. The use of these political connections as a means of privatizing formerly state-owned media assets ultimately resulted in the undermining of the broader reform process.

This last point can be generalized and lends further support to the argument against government intervention to correct for perceived market failures. As we discussed in detail in Chapter 3, the media in many developing countries suffers from an array of direct and indirect government manipulation. Our case studies provided clear examples of these types of manipulation. In many developing countries, political institutions lack strong checks and balances to prevent the abuse of power. Indeed, the lack of fully developed checks is a key reason why a free media is important as a monitoring device on political actors. Where effective checks and balances are absent, there is a greater likelihood that political pressures will influence the behavior of political actors. It is not difficult to envision a situation where attempts by government to correct market failures suffer from "capture" whereby regulations and interventions serve narrow interests at the expense of citizens' broader interests. Indeed, this is the very situation illustrated by the Reformers' Dilemma framework. Where capture does exist, government interventions will reinforce the status quo and significantly weaken the media as a solution to the Reformers' Dilemma. Continued economic stagnation will be the result.

Thus, even if market failures associated with a totally unregulated media industry create some inefficiency when compared to the hypothetical world characterized by economic models of perfect competition, the social costs of remedying these "failures" in terms of overall human and economic development, especially in the developing world, are very likely to trump those created by market imperfections by a wide margin. In very intuitive terms, giving government greater control over the media in developing countries where institutional checks on government behavior are weak or non-existent and corruption and other forms of political abuse are consequently rampant, is like giving a weapon to a violent criminal. The claim that doing so will empower such governments to alleviate media-related market failures is hardly sufficient consolation for the increased political ignorance, apathy, capacity for government abuse, and lower human and economic development that the foregoing chapters and previous research shows greater government control of the media creates.

SUMMATION

This book's overarching argument is that the media is a critical ingredient in the recipe for economic development. Further, the first-best situation is a media free and independent from government control and manipulation. A free media contributes to the process of economic development as a check on political actors and as a mechanism of policy and institutional change. The media should not be seen as something that can be centrally planned or managed either by government officials within the developing country or by policymakers in international development organizations. The emergence of an independent media is not something that needs to be overseen and managed by politicians and bureaucrats. Instead, the goal should be the creation of an environment in which a free and independent media can evolve and sustain.

We have provided clear steps to initiate the process of creating such an environment. A free media is not a guarantee of successful economic development and should be seen as a necessary, but not sufficient, condition for progress. However, a free media does offer an important solution to the Reformers' Dilemma and provides developing countries with the possibility of adopting reforms and institutions conducive to sustainable economic development.

NOTES

1. For some of the potential problems with implementing this method of privatization, see Anderson (2004: 119–120).
2. On the economic benefits of free trade see Bhagwati (2002, 2004). On the cultural benefits of free trade see Cowen (2002) and Jones (2006). On the moral benefits associated with free trade see Friedman (2005).
3. The free-rider problem stems from the fact that a public good is non-excludable. Because of this characteristic, individuals will have an incentive to free ride off the contributions of others. Pricing issues stem from the fact that public goods are non-rivalrous. Once produced, the efficient price of a non-rivalrous good is zero. However, in order for it to be produced in the first place, a positive price must be charged, resulting in the good being undersupplied.
4. For more on the importance of property, prices, and profit and loss for economic calculation, see Mises (1920, 1952).

REFERENCES

Anderson, Robert E. (2004) *Just Get Out of the Way: How Government Can Help Business in Poor Countries*. Washington, DC: Cato Institute.
Baker, C. Edwin (2002) *Media, Markets and Democracy*. Cambridge: Cambridge University Press.

Besley, Timothy and Andrea Prat (2006) "Handcuffs for the Grabbing Hand? Media Capture and Government Accountability," *American Economic Review*, 96: 720–736.

Bhagwati, Jagdish (2002) *Free Trade Today*. Princeton, NJ: Princeton University Press.

Bhagwati, Jagdish (2004) *In Defense of Globalization*. New York: Oxford University Press.

Brown, Allan (1996) "Economics, Public Service Broadcasting, and Social Values," *Journal of Media Economics*, 19(1): 3–15.

Cowen, Tyler (2002) *Creative Destruction*. Princeton, NJ: Princeton University Press.

Flanigan, William and Nancy Zingale (1994) "Political behavior of the American electorate," *Congressional Quarterly*, Washington, DC.

Friedman, Benjamin (2005) *The Moral Consequences of Economic Growth*. New York: Alfred A. Knopf.

Hayek, F.A. (1945) "The Use of Knowledge in Society," *American Economic Review*, 35: 519–530.

Hoskins, Colin, Stuart McFadyen and Adam Finn (2004) *Media Economics: Applying Economics to New and Traditional Media*. Thousand Oaks, CA: Sage Publications.

International Institute for Democracy and Electoral Assistance (2005) http:www.idea.nt.

Jones, Eric L. (2006). *Cultures Merging: A Historical and Economic Critique of Culture*. Princeton, NJ: Princeton University Press.

Ludwig, Johannes (2000) "The Essential Economic Problem of the Media: Working Between Market Failure and Cross-Financing," *Journal of Media Economics*, 13(3): 187–200.

Media Monitoring Agency (2002) "A report on the freedom of speech in Romania," Media Monitoring Agency—Academia Cataverncu.

Mises, Ludwig von (1920 [1975]) "Economic Calculation in The Socialist Commonwealth." In F. A. Hayek (ed.), *Collectivist Economic Planning*, Clifton, NJ: Augustus M. Kelley, pp. 87–130.

Mises, Ludwig von (1944 [1983]). *Bureaucracy*. Grove City, PA: Libertarian Press.

Mises, Ludwig von (1952 [1980]). *Planning for Freedom*. Grove City, PA: Libertarian Press.

Niskanen, William N. (1971) *Bureaucracy and Representative Government*. New York: Aldine, Atherton.

Sen, Amartya (1984) *Poverty and Famines*. Oxford: Oxford University Press.

Sen, Amartya (1999) *Development as Freedom*. New York: Alfred A. Knopf Inc.

Tullock, Gordon (1965) *The Politics of Bureaucracy*. Washington, DC: Public Affairs Press.

Walden, Ruth (2002) 'Insult Laws'. In Alisa Clapp-Itnyre, Roumeen Islam and Caralee McLiesh (eds), *The Right to Tell: The Role of Mass Media in Economic Development*. Washington, DC: The World Bank, pp. 207–324.

Index

Acemoglu, D. 13, 14
advertising 46–7, 68–9, 70
Albarran, A. 7
Ali, O. 54, 70
alternative information
  initial media reforms 158
  preference gap 75
  sources of 75
  see also underground media
Anderson, R. 131
Androunas, E. 124–5

Bagdikian, B. 11
Baker, C. 158, 159
Baker, P. 128
Banisar, D. 53, 54, 55
Barro, R. 85, 105
Bartels, L. 7
Becker, J. 126, 127, 129
Bejarano, R. 120
belief systems 15, 16, 34, 38
Belin, L. 129
Benn, D. 123, 124
Berezovsky, B. 125, 126, 130
Berlusconi, S. 43
Besley, T. 8, 9, 42, 49, 73, 79, 100, 153
black market media see underground
  media
Blair, J. 60
Boettke, P. 15, 122
Bowen, S. 2
Bożyk, P. 108
Brians, C. 7
Brown, A. 158
Burgess, R. 8, 9, 42, 49, 79, 100

Calderón, F. 118
Carrington, T. 45, 53, 65, 67, 68, 69,
  70, 108, 124, 128, 139
Chang, J.-H. 47
Chavez, H. 48

check on government
  media's role as 1, 2, 6, 34, 38, 149,
    164
  studies on 8–9
Chomsky, N. 11
Chong, D. 81, 88
citizens establishing limitations on
  government
  coordination problem 35
Cobden, R. 64
consumer demand and media content
  65–7, 70, 74, 150
coordination mechanism
  media's role as 2–3, 18–19, 32–6
Coyne, C. 15, 18, 39, 75, 79
credibility of information 50, 72–3, 151
crony capitalism 130, 131, 153

David, P. 15
de Soto, H. 31
Denzau, A. 15, 16
deregulation of the media
  early in reform process 144
determinants of media effectiveness 41,
    42, 75
  economic factors 64, 70–71, 73
    advertising 68–9, 70
    consumer demand and media
      content 65–7, 70, 74
    correlation between media
      strength and economic health
      67
    foreign investment in media
      industry 70–71, 73, 74
  government manipulation of the
    media 42–52, 72–3
  legal environment 52, 59–60
    contributing to punctuated
      change 60
    protection of journalists and
      media employees 55–9, 60, 73